# CAPE BRETON

## A FIELD GUIDE TO ADVENTURE

PAT O'NEIL

Nimbus Publishing Limited
PO Box 9301, Station A
Halifax, NS B3K 5N5
(902) 455-4286

Designed by Kathy Kaulbach, Halifax
Printed and bound in Canada

Photo credits: Nova Scotia Economic Development and Tourism pp. 1, 27, 33, 37,104, 132; ECBC/ ACOA Cape Breton pp. 2, 6, 9, 84, 123, 124, 127, 158; E. Beaton Collection, Beaton Institute, U.C.C.B., Sydney, pp. 14, 150; Warren Gordon, Sydney, pp. 23, 70, 94; Owen Fitzgerald, Sydney, pp. 49, 54, 90; Eleanor Thomas Donkin Collection, Beaton Institue, U.C.C.B., Sydney, p. 61; Jack Stephens Collection, Beaton Institute, U.C.C.B., Sydney, p.99 (top); Ken O'Neil, Sydney, pp. 99 (bottom), 101, 112, 118, 140.

Canadian Cataloguing in Publication Data

O'Neil, Pat, 1946-
Explore Cape Breton
Includes index.
ISBN 1-55109-085-6
1. Cape Breton Island (N.S.)—Guidebooks. I. Title.
FC2343.2.064 1994 917.16'9044 C94-950093-3
F1039.C2064 1994

# CONTENTS

**INTRODUCTION** .................................... **1**
Some Island Geography ................................ 2
A Little History ............................................ 4
Using the Book ............................................ 6
Some Special Notes ...................................... 7

**WEST REGION** ...................................... **11**
A Day Trip to Port Hood Island .................. 12
Egypt Falls .................................................. 17
Beaches of the West .................................... 21

**NORTH REGION** .................................. **25**
Craft Studio Tour St. Ann's Bay .................. 26
North River Trail and Waterfall .................. 32
A Walk Along Aspy Bay: Cabot Landing ..... 37
Looking for Gold at Tarbotvale ................... 41
A Visit to a "Cold Spot" at Tarbotvale ......... 46
Uisge Ban Falls ........................................... 49
Red River Trail ............................................ 53
Beaches of the North .................................. 57

**EAST REGION** ...................................... **59**
Old French Mine Site, Port Morien ............. 60
Fossil Hunting at Schooner Cove ................ 66
Lighthouse Trail: A Walk Through History ..................................................... 70
A Bird Walk Along Cape Perce ................... 76
Three Coastal Hikes:
Main-a-Dieu ................................................ 85
Baleine ........................................................ 87
Gooseberry Cove ......................................... 89
Beaches of the East ..................................... 93

**SOUTH REGION** .................................. **97**
A Day at Marble Mountain ......................... 98
Digging Clams at Fuller's Bridge ............... 104
Overnight Camping at Framboise ............. 109
Hike to Fox Cove Near Framboise ............ 114

A Walk Around Crichton Island .............. 118
A Road Tour of Isle Madame .................... 123
Beaches of the South ................................ 130

**CENTRAL REGION ............................. 135**
A Walk to the Caves at Cape Dauphin ...... 136
Through the Brook to MacIntosh Falls...... 140
History Walk Through Sydney's North End ............................................. 145
Beaches in the Central Part of the Island ................................................. 153

**HIKING IN CAPE BRETON HIGHLANDS NATIONAL PARK ............................... 156**

**DIGGING UP YOUR CAPE BRETON ROOTS ................................................ 160**

**INDEX**
By Location ............................................. 165
By Type of Activity ................................. 167

To Ken,
Daniel and Kate

ACKNOWLEDGEMENTS

I would like to thank the following for their assistance: Bertie and Shirley Smith, Port Hood; Bob and Ann Greer, Tarbotvale; Jessie Mae Smith, Tarbot; Beatrice MacNeil, East Bay; John Hanratty and staff of the *Cape Bretoner;* Frank Deschepper, Sydney; Ken MacDonald, Port Morien; Fenton Eisner, Sydney; John Johnston, Sydney; Cathy Murrant, Port Morien; Andre Crepeau, Sydney; the guys, Sydney; Allister and Isabel MacPhail, Marble Mountain; Michael and Carolyn MacKinnon, Framboise; Richard Meuller, Dartmouth; Linda O'Neil, Halifax; Yvon Samson, Petit-de-Grat; Jim St. Clair, Mull River; The Baldners, Antigonish; Sherry MacArthur, E.C.B.C./ACOA; Warren Gordon, Sydney; Owen Fitzgerald, Sydney.

***To the visitor Cape Breton is a distilled essence of loveliness. Its roads run like a song through valleys and glens and beside the tree-shadowed expanse of countless bays.***

—Dorothy Duncan, *Bluenose: A Portrait of Nova Scotia,* 1942

In essence this book is an invitation. It's an invitation to anyone who has ever crouched in a meadow to watch the antics of a nesting bobolink, or crawled into a thicket of ferns for a closer look at the season's first lady's-slipper. It's an invitation to everyone who has happily passed an afternoon strolling along a deserted beach or hiking up the side of a mountain for a picnic.

And most of all, it's an invitation to those who have never done any of those things. Archaeologists say people have been exploring the island of Cape Breton since 6,000 B.C. The Mi'kmaqs have hunted and fished and travelled here for a thousand years. And visitors have been "stopping off" even before

John Cabot erected a cross on the shores of Aspy Bay, in 1497, and claimed the island for the King of England.

And still, down every trail, along every inlet and bay, and beside every waterfall, discoveries are being made, not only by visitors and travellers from other lands, but by those of us who have walked the trails and beaches countless times. Cape Breton is like that.

## SOME ISLAND GEOGRAPHY

One of the most captivating features of our island is its geography. Because Cape Breton is an island, we are surrounded by beaches—rugged beaches and sandy beaches, beaches flanked by sandstone cliffs, and beaches steeped in history.

Whether you're a swimmer or a sunbather, a beachcomber or a nature lover, knowing that the sea—and the beach—are close at hand, whichever way you turn, is a comfort and, well...a luxury.

From the jagged coasts of places like Gabarus and Point Michaud, to the all but deserted sand dunes of Dingwall and Mabou Harbour, to the much-used family beaches at Domin-

*Beyond the beaches are the mountains.*

ion and Mira Gut, the shores of the Atlantic sprawl around us like sunshine on a summer day. We can pass an afternoon basking in the beauty of Belfry Beach, join the swimmers at North Bay, or drift back in time at history-steeped Aspy Bay. We can stroll for hours

## Cape Breton Island

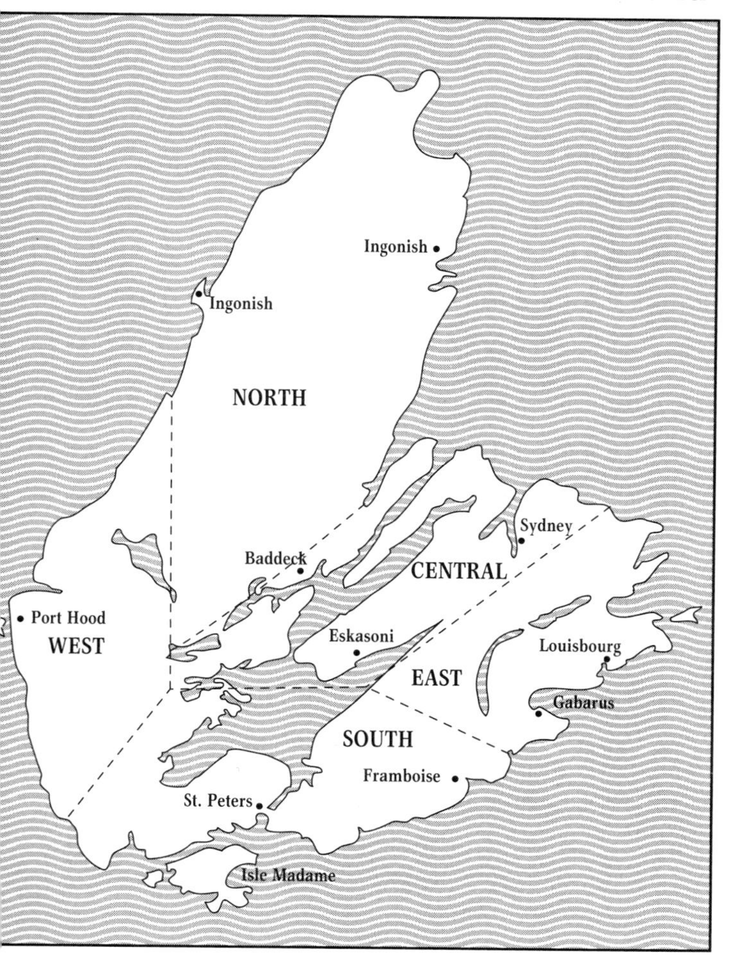

along Main-à-Dieu Passage, collect till our pockets are full along the shores of Isle Madame, and look for fossils at Donkin. Still, we won't even have scratched the surface of what there is to experience along the beaches of Cape Breton.

Beyond the beaches are the mountains. We have mountains that serve as protection from the ocean, like Mabou Ridge, mountains that arise out of the ocean, like Cap Rouge and Smokey, and a mountain made of marble. We have virgin forests, which have stood for hundreds of years. There are rolling fertile farmlands, meadows alive with wildflowers and plants, and barrens where nothing grows except bracken and blueberries.

In the midst of it all is a natural treasure the likes of which you'll find nowhere else on earth—Bras d'Or Lake. From East Bay near Sydney, to West Bay near Port Hawkesbury, the great salt water lake stretches almost the entire length of the Island, sharing with us its crystal water, secluded bays and inlets, glorious beaches, fascinating natural habitats, and breathtaking scenery.

## A LITTLE HISTORY

Fascinating too is Cape Breton's history. When explorer John Cabot first set foot on the beach at Aspy Bay on the northern tip of the island, he may have assumed, as Neil Armstrong probably did when he landed on the moon, that the ground on which he planted his flag was being walked on for the first time. Neil Armstrong may have been right (That remains to be seen!) but John Cabot was not. Not by a long shot! In fact, he could very well have been watched as he erected his cross and raised the flag of St. George. The Mi'kmaqs had been hunting and fishing and camping here for five hundred years before John Cabot arrived, and even before that Vikings are said to have stopped off here on their transatlantic voyages.

And if the thought of Mi'kmaqs and Vikings roaming the island a thousand years ago isn't interesting enough, think back to around the year 6,000 B.C. when archaeologists say that Cape Breton was inhabited by other Indian tribes from Europe

Most of the coastline of Cape Breton is alive with history. In some places it's out in the open for all to see. At the Fortress of Louisbourg, for instance, you can mingle with eighteenth century peasants and noblemen, walk their streets, and eat their food. In Baddeck, at the Alexander Graham Bell Museum, you come to know the man and feel the impact of his achievements. But a lot of the history of the island—unintentionally, for the most part—is not quite so accessible. Tucked away on the shelves of tiny community museums, or rattling around in the heads of would-be historians, much of our intriguing past is one of our best-kept secrets.

With the help of this book, some of these little-known tales of days gone by will come to life for you as you roam the fields of Port Morien or stroll along the seacoast at Lighthouse Point or Kennington Cove.

And I hope that *Explore Cape Breton* will help you to come to know our island for what it truly is—a virtually unspoiled cache of natural, historical, and cultural treasures that will, given great respect and care, remain so for many generations to come.

# USING THE BOOK

*Explore Cape Breton* is a collection of recreational activities, ranging from a challenging 18 km (11.1 mi) hike up a river, to a leisurely driving tour around Isle Madame, to a step-by-step guide to tracing your Cape Breton roots. It is designed as an easy-to-use "take-along" guide that will fit into most knapsacks, pouches, and pockets.

Each activity in the book has a separate entry consisting of a narrative, locator map, directions, and a "quick reference" guide. The quick reference provides useful details like what to wear or bring, time required, distances, etc.

*Hiking in Northern Cape Breton.*

In order to make *Explore Cape Breton* as user friendly as possible, the activities are organized and indexed in the following three ways:

**By Region** The map of Cape Breton (page 3) has been divided into five parts: north, south, east, west, and central. Activities are arranged in the book according to which region they fall into and are listed at the beginning of each section. Some of the island's many beaches are listed at the end of each regional section.

**By Type of Activity** On pages 167-70 you will find all the activities listed again, this time according to "type of activity"—for instance, walks, waterfalls, etc.

**Alphabetically by Location** On pages 165-67 there is a complete list of activities by location, listed alphabetically according to the town, village, or community in which they are located.

In addition to the "activity" section, there is a separate section on Hiking Trails in the Cape Breton Highlands National Park and a concluding section, called "Digging Up Your Cape Breton Roots," which offers advice to those wishing to trace their genealogy on the Island.

## SOME SPECIAL NOTES

Here are some points to ponder before you undertake any of the outdoor activities suggested in this book. Keep in mind that many aspects of nature are very fragile; it is essential that we take great care not to alter or destroy them. By following a few simple guidelines, we can all enjoy outdoor recreation that is environmentally friendly. I urge you also to heed the safety precautions that you will find in the Quick Reference list accompanying each activity.

Here are some pointers:

**Hiking** When hiking stay on established hiking trails if at all possible. Tramping through woods can destroy natural habitats.

**Fires** Build fires only in established fire rings and only when necessary. Be sure fire is extinguished. Check Forest Fire Hazard Index before going into the woods. There are times when not only fires are prohibited, but woods travel itself. Never use live trees for firewood. Even windfalls should be left alone as they are often habitats for living things. Driftwood is acceptable.

**Garbage** Never under any circumstances leave your garbage behind!

**Wildflowers and Plants** Don't pick them! If you have an interest in learning about them, take along your field guides and identify them where they grow. Picking berries that grow along the paths, however, is not harmful, so long as it is done carefully.

**Drinking Water** You are advised not to drink water from streams or rivers unless you know for sure it's safe.

**Beaches** Many ocean beaches with a strong tide or surf develop undertows that can be dangerous to swimmers, especially children. Some beaches have warnings posted; others do not. Be especially careful in a rip tide. You will find some beaches supervised by lifeguards, but the majority of them are not.

**Weather** Cape Breton weather is ... well, interesting. Don't assume that because it's sunny and warm in Mabou, it will be the same story in Port Morien (and vice versa). Be prepared for quick changes, especially along the coast. A foggy day can suddenly break into a scorcher; a calm breeze over Bras d'Or Lake can quickly turn into a gale. You may

*Enjoy an invigorating coastal walk along headlands and cliffs.*

not always like Cape Breton weather, but you'll never be bored with it.

**Cliffs and Rocks** Many coastal walks are along headlands and cliffs high above the rocky shore. Be very careful not to walk close to the edge, as it can be extremely unstable and may crumble under your feet. Watch grassy overhangs that look innocent but are not much more than a thin "shelf" capable of supporting very little weight. Rocks along shore can be slippery, so walk carefully.

**Bird's Nests** If you notice birds flapping and calling hysterically in fields, along a beach, or on a cliff, it usually means there is a nest nearby. Move away as quickly as you can and avoid going near the nest.

**Flies and Bugs** Never underestimate the power of the insect kingdom! It has a way of ruining a perfectly wonderful day. Always take along a good-quality insect repellent, and I suggest taking along a long-sleeved shirt or sweater and long pants, just in case. The good news is that we very often have stiff breezes that keep the little monsters away. If you're walking along the coast, there's not much problem.

**Map Reading** You will notice on each region map two arrows indicating true north and magnetic north. If you were to use a compass you would get a reading for magnetic north. However, because of our position on the globe, magnetic north and true north do not line up—the difference in Cape Breton is about 20 degrees. You probably will never need to be this accurate in your directions, but it is an interesting tidbit of information.

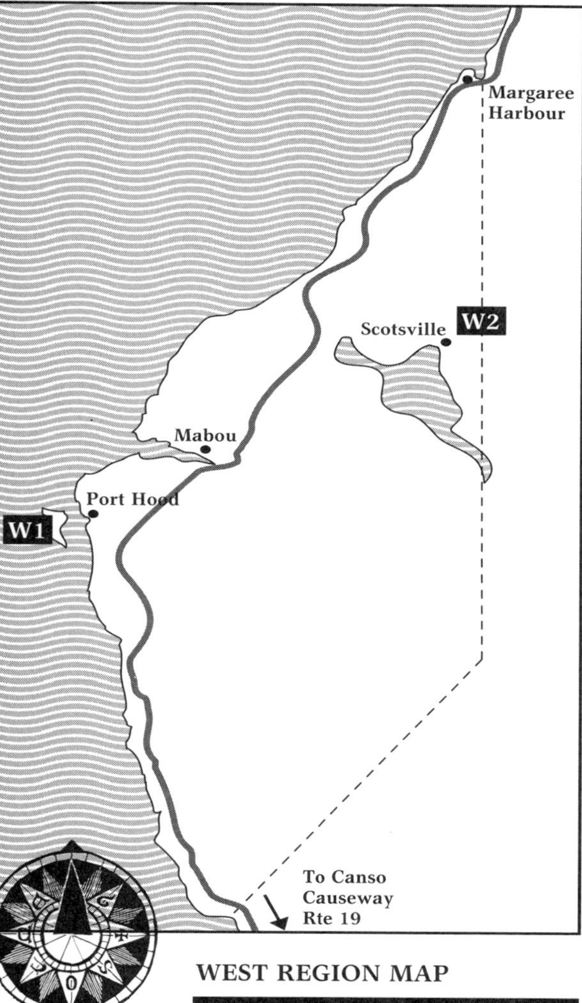


## WEST REGION MAP

**W1** A Day Trip to Port Hood

**W2** Egypt Falls

W1

# A DAY TRIP TO PORT HOOD ISLAND

When Bertie Smith swung his big white "northumberland" away from the dock on Port Hood Island and headed toward the mainland, I twisted in my seat to watch the grey fishing shacks and tidy little houses on the hill grow smaller in the distance. I wanted to stay longer, but it was time to go. I promised myself I'd come back soon. Port Hood Island has that sort of effect on you.

No one knows this better than Bertie Smith. He is the great-great-great-grandson of Captain David Smith of Cape Cod, Massachusetts, who settled the island with his wife and five sons in 1786. For six generations Smiths have lived on "Smith's Island," as it was once called. They've seen fish plants, families, and prosperity come and go. And although it no longer bears their name, much about Port Hood Island—its history and heritage—belongs to the Smiths.

**Port Hood Island**

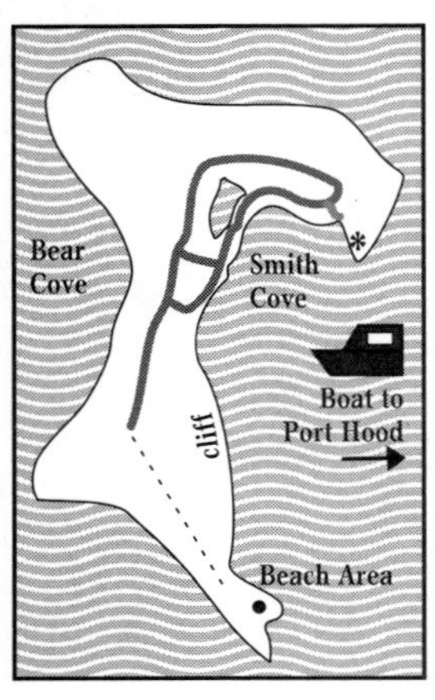


## GETTING THERE

Port Hood Island lies just off the coast from the village of Port Hood, on the west side of Cape Breton. Once you get to Port Hood, find the government wharf (it's between the school and the courthouse) and park your car either on the wharf or along the road. This is where Bertie Smith comes in. He and his wife Shirley are the only permanent residents on the island, and he is available most of the time to ferry you across the bay. I called him the night before (his number is 787-2515), and that seemed to work well for him. But if some day you find yourself on Port Hood wharf, looking longingly across the bay to the island and wishing you had made arrangements for a boat, call Bertie anyway. If he's available, he will come for you. If he isn't, he'll give you the name of someone else who can take you. The fare varies a little according to the number of people, but generally $20.00 round trip is the going rate for four.

**THE ISLAND**

The boat ride is short and pleasant, and as Bertie casually steers his boat across the bay, he'll tell you about his ancestors and his own life on the island—if you ask him. You'll see the shacks and little houses appear on the hillside, then grow to life size as Bertie snuggles the boat into the cove and up against the wharf. He'll help you up the ladder and wish you a good day. From then on, you're on your own.

One of the appealing things about Port Hood Island is its lack of public facilities—no public washrooms, no public telephones, no fast food take-outs. It's wonderful! During the summer months all the houses on the island are occupied, and I'm sure in an emergency any one of the residents would be happy to help out. But if you plan to spend any time there, you must take your own water and food, and anything else you can stuff into a knapsack. Careful—don't take too much! Remember, your only means of getting around is on foot.

The road that leads up from the wharf branches off as it approaches the houses on the hill. Both branches will eventually take you up into the woods and out to the glorious beach at the south end of the island. The

*The Jubilee United Church at Port Hood Island.*

woods are alive with plants, wildflowers, and berries. And don't be surprised if a rabbit or two bounces out in front of you as you walk, or if a deer watches you passing from under a nearby apple tree. My brother-in-law, after his first visit to the island, wrote this about his trip: "We saw a deer, a chipmunk, and several rabbits, all of which seemed not to be wary of human beings—like Paradise before the Fall. In the thick part of the woods there were mosquitoes—like Paradise after the Fall." He's right about one thing: Even with mosquitoes, Port Hood Island does have a certain feel of paradise about it.

If the island church is open, you are welcome to drop in and sign the guest book. There's a pioneer cemetery along the road to

**Activity**
Boat ride to island; hike across island on good road; swim, picnic, nature walk.

**For Whom?**
Suitable for just about anyone, depending on how long you stay. There are no facilities on island for public use, so I wouldn't recommend it for the elderly. Boat ride is short; walking trail is good.

**Conditions and Terrain**
Walking is easy over dirt road; walking along beach is difficult in spots.

**Distances and Times**
Boat ride is about fifteen minutes; walk to end of island (beach) takes about forty-five minutes on the road, longer along the shore. Island is about 4.5 km (2.8 mi) long.

**Best Time of Year**
Summer and fall.

**What to Wear/Bring**
Change of clothes for variable weather; bathing suits and towels, insect repellent, sunscreen, drinking water, food; field guides optional.

**Special Features**
Interesting history, abundant wildlife, birds, and plants; warm swimming water.

**Precautions**
There can be undertows along the channel between the mainland and the island. Keep an eye on children in the water if there is a high sea.

**Facilities**
There are no facilities on the island. Stores, gas stations, etc., on mainland in Port Hood.

the beach. And on the western side of the island (where there's no road) stands a rock quarry, from which rocks were taken by the French to build the Fortress of Louisbourg in the 1700s. If you're up for a bit of a challenge, try walking to the beach along the shore. You'll see fascinating rock formations and lots of fossils.

Whether you spend the whole day or just a few hours on Port Hood Island, I think you'll discover, as I did, what it is that's kept the Smith family on their island for over two hundred years.

**DIRECTIONS**

From the Canso Causeway, drive on the Ceilidh Trail (Route 19) to Port Hood. From Sydney, take the Trans-Canada Highway (Route 105) to Whycocomagh, then take the turnoff to Lake Ainslie and continue until you come to the intersection with Route 252. Take Route 252 to Mabou. Drive west on the Ceilidh Trail to Port Hood.

# EGYPT FALLS

Deep in the hills of Lake Ainslie, where the Matheson Glen Brook runs down to the Southwest Margaree River, there's a trail that hustles you downhill through a magnificent stand of hardwood trees and deposits you face to face with one of the most beautiful waterfalls you will find anywhere. If you're up for a hike with a bit of a challenge, Egypt Falls is an inspiring place to spend a summer afternoon. A friend calls it the "Salem Cigarette Falls." Remember those cigarette ads in the American magazines? It's like that, only better.

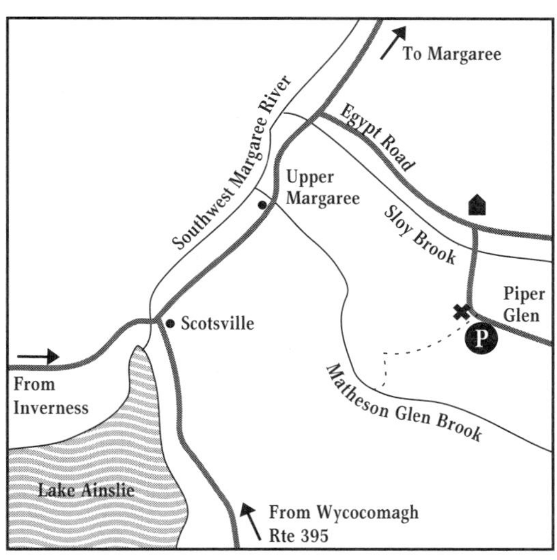


## Egypt Falls

My first trip to Egypt Falls was on a cool, drizzly day in early July, and in spite of the weather I found the surroundings truly unforgettable. The vegetation, as it often is in a Cape Breton wood, is lush and green. Woodland plants, like bunchberry and Solomon's seal, are plentiful, and if you're sharp you may spot a woodland creature that for sure has spotted you. My husband, who doesn't miss much in the woods, pointed out a fat brown partridge perched almost invisibly on the path ahead of us. As we approached, we realized it was a not-so-fat mother puffed up over her five tiny chicks to hide them from danger. They toddled off behind her into the safety of the ferns.

## GETTING TO THE FALLS

The path down to the brook is clearly defined. No fear of getting lost. However, it is very steep, especially the last third of the way. According to the topographical map, the brook is 245 metres (about 800 feet) down from the road. As you approach the bottom, you will need to use the rope railing that has been tied there by, I presume, members of the local communities who want a safe passage to their falls.

Egypt Falls was originally called Appin Falls, and probably still is by some local people. It was named for the Stewart family of Appin, Scotland, who settled near the falls in the 1800s. The area around the falls, Piper Glen, was at one time a school and post office district, but now only a few houses remain.

## DID I MENTION HOW STEEP THE TRAIL IS?

I made two discoveries on my first trip to Egypt Falls—little bonuses for climbing up and down such a steep hill. The first discovery was on the way down. With the hill dipping so aggressively ahead of me, the tops of the tall, elegant birches, pine, and hemlock trees seemed almost to be at eye level. I had

**Activity**

Hike along a steep woodland path to a brook and a waterfall; nature trail and picnic site.

**For Whom?**

Not recommended for the very young or the elderly or anyone with a heart or lung problem.

**Conditions and Terrain**

Path is well defined and easy to follow, but steep. It can be a little muddy in parts after a heavy rain.

**Time Required**

Fifteen minute walk down trail, longer coming back up; the drive, after you turn off at Whycocomagh, will take you about a half hour or so.

**Best Time of Year**

Summer and fall.

**What to Wear/Bring**

Good walking shoes; insect repellent; protective clothing; field guides, picnic optional.

**Precautions**

Keep a lookout for the sign that marks the trail—it is easy to miss. Don't allow children to run downhill. Some of the mushrooms and fungi I found were of the poisonous variety, so be careful!

**Special Features**

Many varieties of trees, plants, flowers, berries, mushrooms, fungi, birds, and wildlife—a nature nut's paradise; falls is a spectacular wall of water.

**Facilities**

Store in Scotsville.

the sensation of walking high in the air among their branches. When I started my uphill climb it was the opposite. The steep incline made me almost parallel to the ground as I climbed, and I could see the forest floor the way a rabbit might see it. I had never realized how fascinating the world was down there—all the jewel-like plants and flowers, intriguing mosses and ground cover, and dozens of strange and sinister-looking mushrooms and fungi. And me without my field guides!

When you make the trip to Egypt Falls, whether it's a grey day in early summer or a brilliant crimson afternoon in October, and whether your field guides are tucked away in your back pocket or your desk drawer, you'll see for yourself what makes it such an unforgettable place, and I predict you'll make some special discoveries of your own.

**DIRECTIONS**

Take the Trans-Canada Highway (Route 105) to Whycocomagh and turn off onto Route 395 North (East Lake Ainslie). Keep on the east side of the lake until you see a sign on the right to Piper Glen and Egypt Road, about 30 km (18.6 mi) from the Whycocomagh turnoff. Turn right and drive about 2 km (1.2 mi). On your left you'll see a small house and across from it is a road with a tiny white bridge. Drive up that road exactly .9 km (.56 mi) and keep a lookout for a small white sign for Egypt Falls. You'll have to keep a sharp eye out for the sign. It's not on the road but partially hidden by vegetation a few yards off to the side, on your right. The trail begins at the sign.

Because the beaches on the west side of the Island border on the Gulf of St. Lawrence, the water is warmer than at most of our other ocean beaches. The coastline here for the most part is less rugged than the north, south, or east shores and broad sandy beaches are plentiful. Be mindful that during a high sea there can be undertows along these beaches, so keep watch over children.

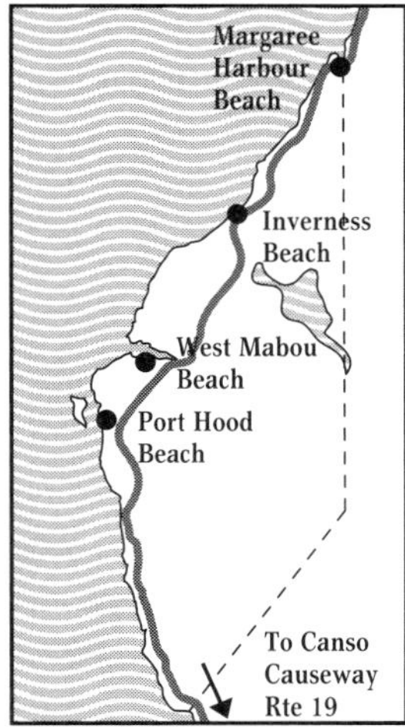


## PORT HOOD BEACH

This is a lovely sandy beach, in view of beautiful Port Hood Island. It is well used by local residents and a great family beach.

### DIRECTIONS

Take the Ceilidh Trail (Route 19) from Port Hawkesbury to Port Hood (51 km [31.6 mi]). Drive through the village and take the wharf road, which is between the school and the courthouse. The beach is next to the wharf.

## WEST MABOU BEACH

The beach here is a very broad expanse of incredible sand dunes and warm harbour water. You can walk for miles along the beach and up along the head of the harbour where it narrows into a channel. A great family outing kind of beach.

### DIRECTIONS

Mabou is 65 km (40.3 mi) northeast of Port Hawkesbury on the Ceilidh Trail (Route 19). Just before you come to the village of Mabou, you will pass through West Mabou. There you will see a road to Colindale. Take it. When the pavement ends, drive another km (.62 mi) to a narrow road on your right (just past a cedar house). This road will take you to the beach.

## INVERNESS BEACH

This is a sprawling stretch of wonderful sandy beach on the shore of the Northumberland Strait. Since it's so open, sea breezes tend to prevail, and the water is colder than at Mabou Harbour or Port Hood. It's a wonderful place to beachcomb or just walk.

### DIRECTIONS

The town of Inverness is on the Ceilidh Trail (Route 19), 86 km (53.3 mi) northeast of Port Hawkesbury. The road to the beach runs down towards the water from the west end of town.

## MARGAREE HARBOUR BEACH

This is a wonderful beach for family outings and picnics, and a good place for children to play as the water slopes gradually from the shore. The water warms up quite nicely by midsummer.

*Margaree Harbour Beach, a great place for family outings.*

### DIRECTIONS

You can reach Margaree Harbour by driving along the Ceilidh Trail (Route 19) through Mabou and Inverness. It's about 30 km (18.6 mi) northeast of Inverness. Drive through Inverness, keeping left at Dunvegan, until you pass Chimney Corner and Whale Cove. Margaree Harbour road is on your left about

2.5 km (1.5 mi) from the Whale Cove Summer Village.

You can also approach Margaree Harbour by taking the Cabot Trail north through Margaree Forks. It is 64 km (39.7 mi) north of Baddeck. From Margaree Forks drive along the west side of the Margaree River. When you come to the intersection of the Cabot Trail and the Ceilidh Trail, just before the long causeway, turn left (this is known as the Shore Road) and drive about 1 km (.62 mi) to another intersection. Turn right. This is the Margaree Harbour Road. It ends at Laurence's General Store where you can stock up on anything you might need for an impromptu picnic. Park your car just beyond the store and walk down over the sand dunes to the beach.

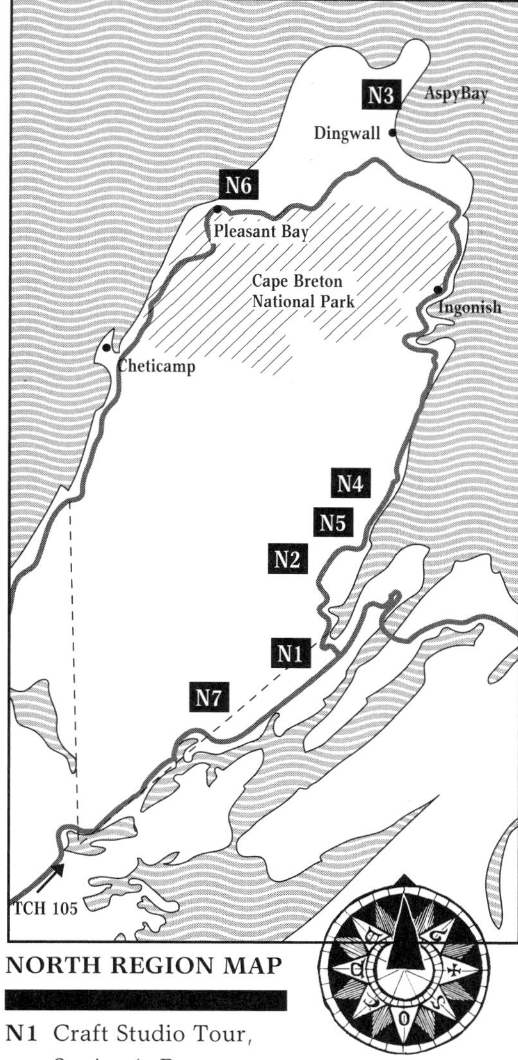


## NORTH REGION MAP

**N1** Craft Studio Tour, St. Ann's Bay
**N2** North River Trail and Waterfall
**N3** A Walk Along Aspy Bay
**N4** Looking for Gold at Tarbotvale
**N5** Visit to a Cold Spot at Tarbotvale
**N6** Uisage Ban Falls
**N7** Red River Trail

N1

# CRAFT STUDIO TOUR ST. ANN'S BAY

***Penetrating into an elevated country...[St. Ann's] harbour presents the most majestic scenery of any in Cape Breton.***

—T.C. Haliburton, *An Historical and Statistical Account of Nova Scotia,* 1829

**St. Anns Bay**

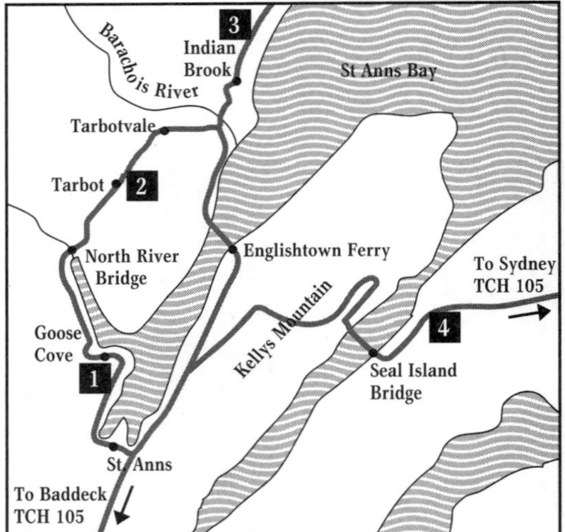


1 Goose Cove Pottery
2 Wild Things wood carvings
3 Leather Works
4 Quilts and Weaving

If you're interested in a first-hand glimpse of some of Cape Breton's finest artisans at work, I suggest a leisurely afternoon tour around St. Ann's Bay.

What you will find there along that 40 km (24.8 mi) stretch of the Cabot Trail, aside from some of the most historic and captivating ocean views on the island, is a blend of artistry and craftsmanship as enticing as the Cape Breton landscape itself.

You're invited to watch the creative hands of potter Carole MacDonald at Goose Cove Pottery, see Claire Ryder and Juan Prieto work their magic on wood at Wild Things in

*From the many bays, inlets and harbours, to the lakes and rivers, you're never far from water.*

Tarbot, stop off and chat with leather craftsman John Roberts about his historic reproductions, and drop in to look over the expertly crafted quilts and weaving of Gavinna MacKenzie at Seal Island. They all welcome visitors and are happy to talk about the technique and character of their work.

## ON THE ROAD TO GOOSE COVE POTTERY

Your tour around the bay begins at Goose Cove, about 6 km (3.7 mi) north of the Trans-Canada Highway, on the Cabot Trail. Turn off the Trans-Canada at St. Ann's and drive north until you see the sign for Goose Cove Pottery. You'll find the studio up the driveway, behind the house, and that's where you'll usually find Carol MacDonald throwing, glazing, or firing some of her distinctive pots. Carol produces both porcelain and stoneware pottery (She can explain the difference) and her designs reflect her truly creative nature.

If you've never heard of "raku," you will when you visit Goose Cove. This sixteenth-century Japanese process of firing clay is a speciality there, and you'll be fascinated by the "lusters, crackles, and surprises" created when the pots, red hot from the kiln, are placed in combustible material and deprived of oxygen. Even Carol herself can't predict what her raku pieces will look like until the process is complete. Along with the raku and Carol's other porcelain and stoneware pottery, you'll find a selection of other crafts and gifts. The studio and shop are open from 9 A.M. to 5 P.M., seven days a week, from mid-June until Labour Day.

## NORTH TO "WILD THINGS"

From Goose Cove, continue driving north, across the North River Bridge and around the head of the bay. On your way you may want to stop off at the School On the Hill craft shop, just over the bridge on your left.

About 7 km (4.3 mi) from Goose Cove you'll come to Tarbot and the sign "Wild

Things." This isn't a wildlife park, it's the woodcraft studio owned by Claire Ryder and Juan Prieto. When you see their work, you'll understand how the studio got its name.

The wood turnings and carvings created at Wild Things, although elegantly shaped and polished, retain the wild spirit of the wood, and Claire and Juan are passionate about allowing that wild spirit to guide their skillful hands as each piece of wood takes shape on their lathe. The wood is meticulously selected and carefully dried: driftwood delicately tinted by the sea; a blackened piece of oak from a ship long lost in some Atlantic gale; a windfall, partially decayed and deeply hued by a fungus; roots, dead wood, and green wood all have a place on Claire and Juan's lathe. Each piece is truly unique, and I guarantee that you'll be enchanted by the wild things and Wild Things.

**LEATHER WORKS**

Continue your northward trek until you come to the intersection at the Barachois Bridge, about 4 km (2.5 mi) from Tarbot. Turn left there and continue on the Cabot Trail for another 5 km (3 mi) to John Robert's Leather Works. You may already have seen some of John's work at Fortress Louisbourg, or Fort Ann in Annapolis Royal. His leather reproductions, mostly eighteenth and nineteenth century handstitched fire buckets and soldiers' accoutrement, are works of art. Ask John, too, about his "flower bags." They look like soft leather pouches, but they're not. Through a process called *cuir bouili,* the vegetable tanned leather is soaked in hot water, then shaped and left to harden. You'll find samples of other local crafts at Leather Works as well. Drop in any day, Monday through Sunday from 9 A.M. to 5 P.M., from the beginning of May to the beginning of October.

**TO SEAL ISLAND AND GAVINNA MACKENZIE'S QUILTS AND WEAVING**

Your last stop is at the home of quilter and weaver Gavinna MacKenzie at Seal Island. To get there you'll have to backtrack a little. Turn around and head back south until you come again to the Barachois Bridge. Keep straight through onto Route 312 to the Englishtown Ferry. Cross on the ferry, drive a few kilometres up to the Trans-Canada Highway (Route 105) and turn left, up and over Kelly's Mountain. Cross the Seal Island Bridge, and when you come to the Ross Ferry Road on your right (just before the Cedar House Restaurant), you'll see an older style farmhouse on your left with a green mailbox.

That's where you'll find Gavinna MacKenzie. She welcomes visitors any time and chances are you'll find her behind the big loom weaving, or stitching away on another quilt masterpiece. She'll show you beautiful hand-woven blankets, place mats and floor mats, and the elegant quilts that she creates with the help of a church group that meets there regularly. The quilts and woven pieces are for sale, of course, and I'm sure Gavinna would be happy to take orders for any special requests.

This tour of working artisans studios around St. Ann's Bay is just a small sample of the artistry you'll find in craft studios all around Cape Breton. Tourist Information Centres will have brochures and information on shops and studios in other parts of the island.

**DIRECTIONS**

From the Trans-Canada Highway (Route 105) take the Cabot Trail north at St. Ann's (road is next to Lobster Galley Restaurant).

ST. ANNS • QUICK REFERENCE

**Activity**

A driving tour with stops at four working craft studios and gift shops.

**For Whom?**

Anyone.

**Time Required**

Give yourself at least two hours, but you'll find lots to keep you on the road longer.

**Time of Year**

Summer and early fall.

**Facilities**

Restaurant at St. Ann's; gas stations, restaurants, and accommodations at Seal Island.

N2

# NORTH RIVER TRAIL AND WATERFALL

When I went looking for the North River Trail, at the head of St. Ann's Bay, I had no idea what to expect. A picnic site, I was told, with a "trail of some sort."

What I found was a most pleasant surprise. The picnic park itself is a sprawling well-cared-for provincial site with picnic tables, drinking water, and toilet facilities. The "trail of some sort" turned out to be a wonderful 9 km (5.6 mi) (18 km return) hiking trail that follows the North River upward to a spectacular 30.5 m (100 ft) waterfall, complete with lofty lookoff.

We set out on the trail that day, my friend and I, with high hopes of reaching the waterfall with enough daylight left for the hike back. After four or five kilometres (2.5 to 3 mi) the sun began to fade slowly behind us into the evergreens, and we were beginning to feel the effects of our too-meagre lunch. Reluctantly we decided to turn back, but vowed to return—earlier in the day and with more food in our knapsack.

## LITTLE FALLS

When you drive into the park, you'll see to your right a sign and map for the river trail. If you don't plan to make the journey all the way upriver to the Big Falls, you might want to scoot down to see the Little Falls. Just to the left of the sign there's a fisherman's path that leads down to the river. It's about a fifteen-minute walk each way and you'll find a delightful little waterfall at the end.

*After a day of adventure, enjoy a secluded picnic lunch.*

**BIG FALLS**

If you prefer to get right down to business and see the Big Falls, just take the path that leads into the woods beside the sign.

Don't be alarmed at the steepness of the first part of this trail. This section is just a connector path to get you onto the main trail. When you reach the end of this path, turn left onto the main trail that takes you up the river.

The first few kilometres of the main trail is actually an old road. I was surprised to discover that this area, over a hundred years ago, was a settlement of several families of Highland Scot descent. It's a little difficult to imagine a time when this wild woodland rang with the laughter of children on their way to the school, which was located, along with a tannery, at the entrance to the park. Can you picture cattle grazing in a nearby pasture or homespun clothes snapping in a summer

## North River Trail

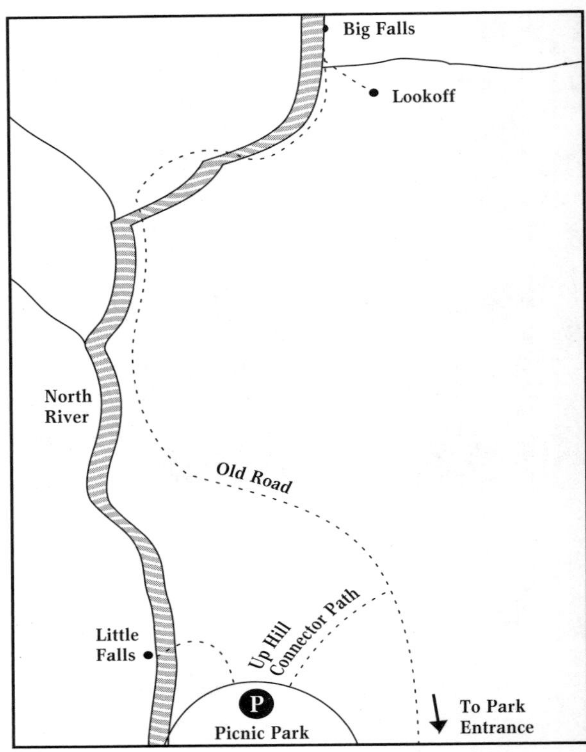


breeze on a backyard clothesline? If you look, you'll see the occasional remnant of a rock fence or foundation—the only reminders of those steadfast homesteaders of long ago.

**THE TRAIL**

After you walk the short connector path and step onto the main trail, make a mental note where to pick up the path again on your way back. When I was there two orange ribbons marked the spot, but you can't count on them always being there and they are easily missed on your walk back. If you do happen to miss the connecting path coming back, don't panic. The road will soon lead you out to the park entrance. Just turn right and walk up the park road to your car.

The first third of the trail is a truly delightful woodland walk that will take you through some of Cape Breton's finest natural habitats for wild plants, birds, and small animals. A detour down any one of the salmon pool paths, which you'll see along the way, will take you to the river bank, where salmon literally leap out of the water (at least they did the day I was there!). If anglers are fishing, be quiet. You don't want to spook the fish.

As you continue along upriver, the road tapers to a trail, and you will happily find yourself walking in full view of the river. In fact, you'll twice cross the river via newly constructed footbridges. The falls, so I'm told, is a magnificent sight, either from the trail or from the lookoff about 1 km (.62 mi) uphill from the trail.

Whether you see the Big Falls upriver, or the Little Falls just down over the hill, you'll find whatever time you spend at North River a memorable experience.

## DIRECTIONS

From the Trans-Canada Highway (Route 105), turn off onto the Cabot Trail at St. Ann's (next to the Lobster Galley Restaurant) and drive north to North River. Cross the bridge and turn left onto the Oregan Road. Drive about 3 km (1.9 mi) (Keep to your left) until you come to the sign for the Provincial Park. Turn at the sign and drive into the park until the road ends.

NORTH RIVER • QUICK REFERENCE •

**Activity**
Hike through woods and along North River to a 30.5 m (100 ft) waterfall.

**For Whom?**
Not recommended for the elderly as there are some steep climbs.

**Conditions and Terrain**
Steep climb for first part, then good walking along an old road tapering to a good trail; there are footbridges across streams and river; trail is maintained by the Province of Nova Scotia.

**Distances**
Eighteen km (11.2 mi) return to Big Falls; less than 1 km (.62 mi) to Little Falls.

**Time Required**
About seven hours to waterfall and back; about thirty minutes return to Little Falls.

**What to Wear/Bring**
Good walking shoes, preferably long sleeves and pants; insect repellent; food, and drinking water; field guides optional.

**Precautions**
Leave enough daylight to get back.

**Special Features**
Beautiful vistas along the river; 30.5 m (100 ft) waterfall with lookoff; wild flowers, plants, and birds.

# A WALK ALONG ASPY BAY: CABOT LANDING

When John Cabot, aboard the *Matthew*, dropped anchor in Aspy Bay over 500 years ago, he was looking for a western route to the Orient. My theory is that he was so mesmerized by the splendour of Aspy Bay, he forgot all about the Orient, planted his cross on that beautiful shore, and went home a happy man.

It must be a wonderful sight to sail into Aspy Bay on a brilliant June day with the ivory beaches stretching around you like a welcome and the white gypsum cliffs, Sugar Loaf, and the lofty Capstick Mountains all spread out before you to feast your eyes upon.

But seeing Aspy Bay from the ocean is only one way to experience its splendour. Luckily, no matter where you go on land along that incredible shore you'll be treated to white cliffs and high mountain vistas, wild ocean and silent ponds, seabirds and eagles soaring, and a feeling that you want to stay forever.

*If you're inclined to walk, Cabot Beach is an open invitation.*

**WALK THE BEACH**

If you're inclined to walk, this beach is an open invitation. There's a 3 km (1.9 mi) strip of land that stretches from the picnic park out along the ocean to a narrow channel that runs into a large, still pond called North Pond. Beyond the pond, reaching over three hundred metres (a thousand feet) to the sky, sprawls Sugar Loaf and the mountain ridge that seems

**Aspy Bay**

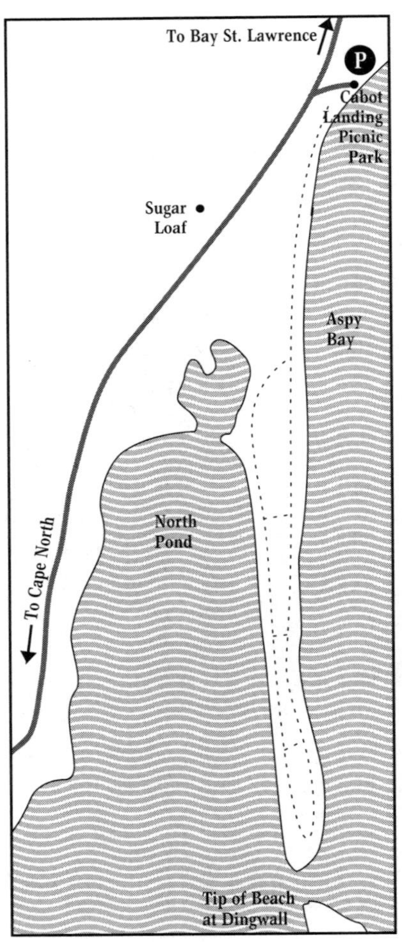

to follow you as you walk. In summer the hills are a glorious sea of dark green conifers and chartreuse hardwoods. In fall they are a spectacle of brilliant red and orange.

As you walk along the beach, the white gypsum cliffs of White Point rise in the distance to greet you, and you will come upon a channel at the very tip that runs from North Pond into the ocean. Just across the channel you'll see the northerly tip of the beach at Dingwall (see page 57).

On your walk back from the point, you may want to try walking behind the beach, along the shore of the pond. Be sure to stay close to the water so you won't disturb any habitats in the grass and bushes.

You'll see a couple of paths along the way that will take you back onto the ocean beach. Be careful not to trample the beach grass. It helps keep the sand from blowing off that part of the beach and in spring and summer it provides a nesting ground for small shore birds. Your walk back will give you wonderful views of the northern head of the bay and the hills of Bay St. Lawrence.

## A LITTLE SURPRISE

From the picnic park, look up to the mountains just across the road from the park. There on a ledge, about halfway up the mountain, is a very unusual sight.

## DIRECTIONS

From the Cabot Trail, turn off at Cape North toward Bay St. Lawrence. Drive about 18 km (11 mi) until you come to the Cabot Landing Picnic Site. The beach walk is to the right (south) of the picnic site.

ASPY BAY • QUICK REFERENCE

**Activity**
Picnic, swim, walk along barrier beach and salt pond.

**For Whom?**
Can be enjoyed by just about anyone.

**Conditions and Terrain**
Walk is along a well-packed sandy beach; water is cool with long rolling surf.

**Distances**
Picnic Park is 18 km (11 mi) from turnoff at Cape North; beach is about 6.5 km (4 mi) return.

**Time Required**
Walk will take about 1 1/2 hours.

**What to Wear/Bring**
Bathing suits, towels, picnic, sunscreen, insect repellent.

**Time of Year**
For swimming—late July to late September; for walking—anytime in spring, summer, or fall.

**Precautions**
Watch children in water—if surf is high there may be an undertow.

**Facilities**
Picnic tables, toilet facilities, stores in Cape North and Bay St. Lawrence.

# LOOKING FOR GOLD AT TARBOTVALE

N4

This excursion is not for the faint of heart or fragile of limb. If you're looking for a leisurely stroll along a peaceful woodland path, this isn't it.

What this is, really, is an adventure. It's a rugged walk up the Barachois River to a spot that is believed to be the site of a gold strike back in the mid-1800s.

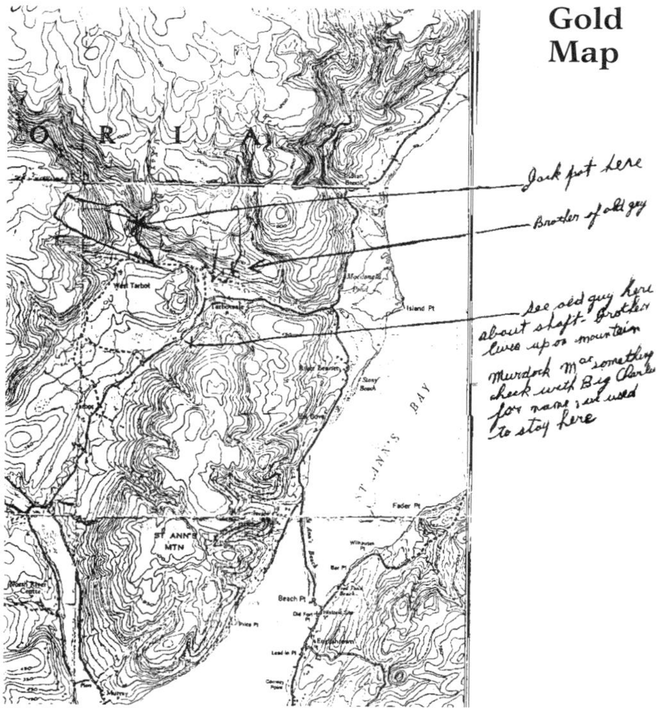


**Gold Map**

About 2 km (1.2 mi) up the Barachois River from Tarbotvale, the MacKay Brook winds down from the mountains and empties into the ocean-bound waters of the river. It's here, over a century and a half ago, that an old prospector, after searching for many years, finally found gold. Local legend has it that the old man staked his claim and sunk a shaft near the intersection of river and brook. And according to my history source—an elderly lady from Tarbot—the prospector was offered $23,000 for his claim. "A lot of money in those days," she reminded me. He refused the offer and managed to dig out for himself a tidy little stash of gold. The story goes that he lost the seam eventually and was never able to pick it up again.

Many other have staked claims over the years hoping to rediscover the seam, but so far as I know it has yet to be found. The map is a copy of the one that was given to me by a resident of Tarbotvale. It's dated 1953, and as you can see by the notations made by a more recent "gold digger," the fever endured for many years.

## A FEW CONSIDERATIONS

Now, before you rush off into the woods of Tarbotvale with your treasure map in hand, there are some things you should know.

First of all, I'm not seriously suggesting that anyone who follows this map will find gold in "them thar hills." And I'm certainly not advocating any sort of digging or tearing up of the forest floor in search of the old mine shaft. For me, this excursion was just a fun outdoor adventure—with a little history and intrigue. The second thing you should consider before you set out is that the journey upriver is not an easy one. The trail, which is a little difficult even to find, deteriorates about halfway up the river into an animal track and eventually disappears altogether. From there you must follow the river bank, which can be overgrown and difficult to negotiate.

If all of that hasn't discouraged you, then you're just the person for the adventure.

## THE JOURNEY UPRIVER

As the map shows, the Barachois River runs down from the hills of St. Ann's and empties into the waters of St. Ann's Bay. The trail along the river is probably a little-used fisherman's path that may even have been used by the prospectors themselves.

Once you cross the bridge at Tarbotvale, drive up the hill a few hundred metres until you see a barn on your right. Park your car in the clearing there and cross the road to the field. Walk through the field (the owner has given his consent), keeping downhill to your left, and you'll see a slight opening in the trees. I had to duck under the branches of two evergreen trees to get to it. The path heads a little downhill into the woods, to your left.

The walking is very pleasant for about the first kilometre (.62 mi) or so; then the going

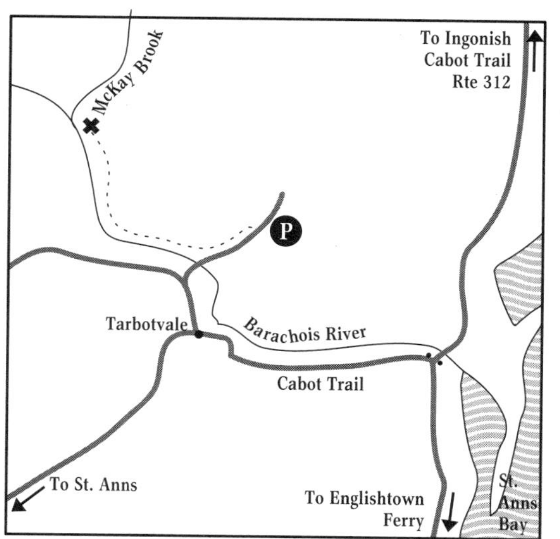


**Tarbotvale Gold Mine**

gets tricky. I was able to follow some blazed trees for another half kilometre or so, but you would be better advised, once you notice the path begin to disappear, to take a short detour down to the river and continue your journey along the river bank or along the edge of the woods. The alders can be quite thick in places, and the windfalls are numerous. Be sure to dress appropriately.

When you've travelled about 2 km (1.2 mi) in all, you'll come upon what looks like a pile of stones on the river bank. Snuggled in behind this landmark is the mouth of the MacKay Brook, where it empties into the Barachois River.

According to the map, this is where "X" marks the spot!

**DIRECTIONS**

Take the Englishtown Ferry (road to ferry is located at the western base of Kelly's Mountain) and drive on Route 312 to the yellow flashing light just before the Barachois Bridge, about 4 km (2.5 mi) from the ferry. Turn left onto the Cabot Trail south and drive 2 km (1.2 mi) to Tarbotvale. Turn right at the sign for the Tarbotvale Soccer Field and Greer's Bed and Breakfast. Drive on that road until you cross the bridge.

**Activity**
A rather difficult hike up a river to a spot where gold was once discovered and mined.

**For Whom?**
This is only recommended for those who don't mind travelling over difficult terrain.

**Conditions and Terrain**
The beginning of the trail is good walking, but it deteriorates and then disappears. The rest of the way is along the edge of the woods and along the river bank.

**Distances**
The site is about 2 km (1.2 mi) from the beginning of the trail.

**Time Required**
At least two hours.

**What to Wear/Bring**
Wear long-legged and long-sleeved clothing, good walking shoes, and insect repellent; picnic optional.

**Time of Year**
Summer and fall.

**Precautions**
Stay close to river; don't dig up or disturb surroundings.

N5

# A VISIT TO A "COLD SPOT" AT TARBOTVALE

If you happen to be driving around St. Ann's Bay on a steamy summer day looking for a spot to cool off, here's an interesting suggestion that doesn't even involve getting wet.

At Tarbotvale turn up the dirt road where you see a sign for the Tarbotvale Soccer Field and Greer's Bed and Breakfast. A short distance up that road, just before the bridge, you'll see another road to your left. Turn onto it and drive for a short distance until you come to a small cabin on your right. Cross the road and walk back a little until you find a path (of sorts) across the ditch and into the woods. Not far in on your right—you'll no doubt feel it before you see it—is what is known as "a cold spot." And a cold spot it is!

**Tarbotvale Cold Spot**

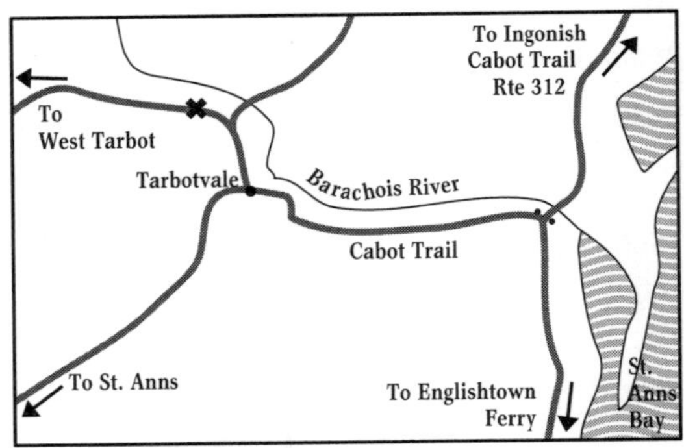


## AN OUTDOOR REFRIGERATOR

Even on the hottest day in summer you will feel a very chilly breeze wafting up from the crevices in the rock. It feels a bit like you just opened the refrigerator door. Touch the inside of the rocks or slip your hand down into the crevices. It's easy to see why, many years ago, the family who homesteaded on this land used this spot as their refrigerator.

I'm told the opening was larger than it is now—more like a little cave—and the temperature was so constant there, summer and winter, that even when "ice boxes" came to Cape Breton, the family chose not to forsake their outdoor larder for the newfangled contraption. The food probably tasted much better stored out in the fresh country air!

## WHAT CAUSES "COLD SPOTS"?

Curiosity aroused, I did a little checking to find out why cold spots happen. It seems that when deep crevices occur in rock such as in the granite at Tarbotvale, water seeps down from the surface into the cracks. When the water in the "caverns" evaporates it produces a cool vapour that rises to the surface. This constant exchange of air—drawing from the outside and sending back the cooled vapour—causes the chilly "breeze" you feel on the surface and keeps the temperature constant inside the cavern.

If you see ice on the rocks around the opening—which you very well might, even in July—it's left over from the winter because the cool air around the rocks and the lack of sunlight in the woods prevents it from melting.

## DIRECTIONS

Take the Englishtown Ferry (road to the ferry is located at the western base of Kelly's Mountain) and drive on Route 312 to the yellow flashing light and the Barachois Bridge—about 4 km (2.5 mi) from the ferry. Turn left onto the Cabot Trail south and drive 2 km (1.2 mi) to Tarbotvale. Turn right where you see the sign for the Tarbotvale Soccer Field and Greer's Bed and Breakfast. Just before you come to the bridge, take the road to your left.

**TARBOTVALE COLD SPOT • QUICK REFERENCE**

**Activity**
A short visit to see a spot that remains cold as a refrigerator all summer.

**For Whom?**
Anyone.

**Conditions and Terrain**
Very short, easy walk into woods on a path.

**Time of Year**
Summer.

## UISGE BAN FALLS



This is an excursion I wish everyone could take. Whenever I have visitors "from away," I make sure Uisge Ban Falls gets a high priority spot on our sightseeing agenda. In summer it's a wonderful hike through a mixed hardwood and conifer forest, alive with wildflowers, berries, mushrooms, and birds. In autumn, when the lush greenery it transformed into a sea of reds and yellows, it is magnificent.

*Uisge Ban Falls*

The name "uisge ban" is Gaelic for "white water" and is pronounced (at least by those of us don't "have the Gaelic") OOSH-KA Ban. The white water, of course, refers to the falls that tumbles down from the sheer rock cliff towering high above you as the trail leads you deep into the valley.

Because the Uisge Ban trails are maintained by the provincial park authority, the walking is excellent and with the exception of a few uphill climbs, suitable for almost everyone. You will find wooden foot bridges, hand railings and rest stops all along the way and the network of trails is such that you can choose to take a shorter walk straight to the falls (called the Falls Trail) or the longer way around via the North Branch of the beautiful Baddeck River (called the River Trail).

## Uisge Ban Falls

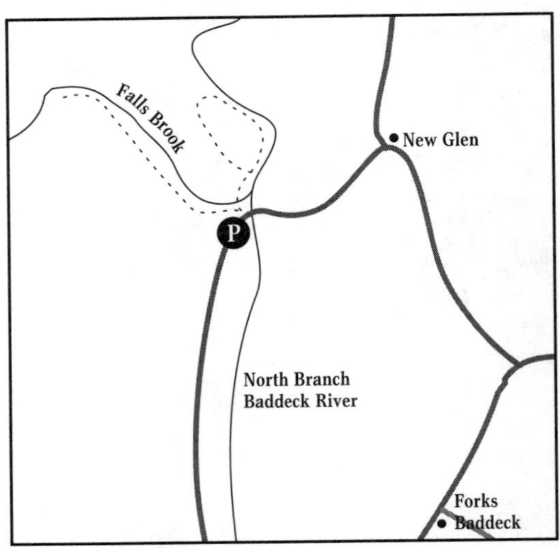


### THE FALLS TRAIL

The Falls Trail carries you gradually up a brook through a pleasant hardwood forest and into a deep stream valley to the falls. When you reach the falls you'll feel the power of the sheer rock cliffs that rise over five hundred feet above you on either side.

**THE RIVER TRAIL**

The River Trail takes you along the banks of the North Branch Baddeck River where you can stop off at one of the lookoffs for a more intimate view. The trail eventually veers away from the river into a glorious climax forest of sugar maples, yellow birch, and beech trees.

The fascinating vegetation and bird life all along the trail, whichever one you choose to take, will put your guide books to good use. I once counted over twenty varieties of mushrooms and fungi in one afternoon. The rest stops and vistas at the falls, in the woods, and along the river will give you many opportunities to sit for a while and take in the potpourri of sights, sounds, and smells that surround you.

**DIRECTIONS**

There are two ways to approach Uisge Ban Falls, one by way of Baddeck Bridge and one by way of Forks Baddeck. As I am familiar with the Forks Baddeck route, I will take you that way.

Take exit 9 off the Trans Canada Highway at Baddeck and follow the sign for Forks Baddeck. Drive along that road, past the golf course, until you have crossed two single-lane bridges. After the second bridge, keep right until you come to a sign for "MacPhee's Cross Road." (You may also see a small sign for the falls.) Turn onto that road and after you've driven about 1 km (.62 mi), you'll come to another intersection (You may see another sign for the falls). Turn left and drive until you come to the parking lot and picnic area, just a few hundred metres away.

USIGE BAN FALLS • QUICK REFERENCE

**Activity**
Woodland hike to a waterfall and along a river.

**For Whom**
Suitable for just about any, except those who can't negotiate uphill climbs (Climbs are quite short, but some are steep).

**Conditions and Terrain**
Walking is good, trails are very well groomed, footbridges, hand railings and lookoff sites all along trail; benches here and there.

**Distances**
Trail to the falls is about 3.5 km (2.2 mi) return, River Trail is about the same. If you walk to the falls along the River Trail, which is a round about way, it is about 5 km return.

**Time**
About two hours to complete both trails.

**What to Wear/Bring**
Walking shoes; field guides, picnic optional.

**Time of Year**
Summer and fall.

**Special Features**
Beautiful river vistas, waterfall, picnic site.

**Facilities**
Picnic tables and toilet facilities at beginning of trail; stores in Baddeck.

# RED RIVER TRAIL



"Just up the road a bit," the old man answered, pointing straight ahead of me. I had stopped to ask if I was on the road to the Red River Trail. Having driven several kilometres, I was beginning to suspect I had taken a wrong turn.

"This is the road alright," he said. "Trail's at the end, just past the monastery."

"Monastery?"

"Yup! Gampo Abbey," he grinned, delighted with my surprise. "Buddhists... been here for quite a while now."

Well, I decided, as I wound my car around the final few kilometres of the Red River road, if it was tranquillity, isolation, and inspiration the monks were seeking, they certainly found it here. I passed the Gampo Abbey sign a short distance up the road, and the temptation to drive in and take a closer look was great. I resisted and satisfied myself with a little rubber-necking as I slowed down to a crawl while passing.

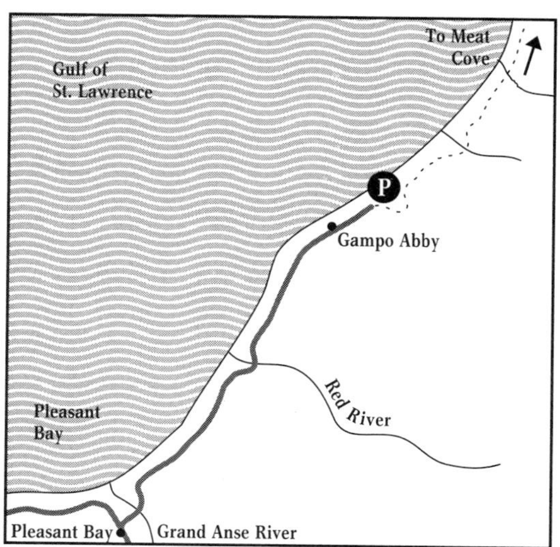


**Red River Trail**

The abbey itself is a wonderfully simple wooden building with many windows looking seaward and small outbuildings scattered around it on the grounds. Tranquillity certainly seemed to reign and I was happy not to have disturbed the silence.

## THE TRAIL

As the old man had said, the trail began where the road ended a very short distance (less than 1 km [.62 mi]) from the Abbey. I parked my car in a little clearing at the end of the road, high above the pounding surf, and looked around until I discovered the path. I found it across the road, heading down along a brook through the woods.

*Enjoy beachcombing, hiking and the awesome views.*

I'm told that the trail—which incidentally is called the Red River Trail in spite of the fact that the Red River is quite a few kilometres back down the road—goes all the way along the coast to Meat Cove, more than 30 km

(18.6 mi) away. It's an old trail used apparently many years ago by a farming family (maybe more than one) who lived at Pollett's Cove, about 10 km (6.2 mi) up along the coast.

Pollett's Cove is a wonderful spot with a glorious beach, acres of old farmland, and two rivers running down into the ocean. Seems like a great place for an overnight camping trip—if you travel light.

If you're not up for a long hike, the Red River Trail is ideal too for short afternoon jaunts. Within just a few kilometres you'll pass through dense northern Cape Breton forest, along tiny brooks heading for the sea, and over rocky cliffs that drop almost perpendicularly below you to the shore. And you may feel, as I do whenever I'm in that part of the island, that you could be walking on top of the world. I'm not sure if it's the elevation or the fact that this is the very northern tip of Cape Breton, but whatever it is, it makes any excursion "down north" a truly memorable event.

## DIRECTIONS

From Cheticamp, follow the Cabot Trail north to Pleasant Bay. Watch for the sign on your left for Red River. From Ingonish, follow the Cabot Trail to Pleasant Bay. Watch for the sign for Red River on your right. Drive 9 km (5.6 mi) to the end of the road. Pavement ends after five km (3.1 mi). You'll see ahead of you a small cabin in the field. Park to the left of the road in the clearing overlooking the water. To your right, across the road, you'll find the path that leads into the woods, then through the field around the back of the cabin, and along the coast.

RED RIVER TRAIL • QUICK REFERENCE •

**Activity**
Walk along the coast and through the woods.

**For Whom?**
Just about anyone who doesn't have trouble negotiating some fairly steep climbs.

**Conditions and Terrain**
Path is well defined but at times further along the trail it can become more difficult to follow; trail is hilly, sometimes through the woods, sometimes on the coast.

**Distances**
Trail begins 9 km (5.6 mi) from the turnoff to Red River at Pleasant Bay; trail stretches about 30 km (18.6 mi) to Meat Cove.

**Time Required**
You can spend as much or as little time as you wish on this trail.

**What to Wear/Bring**
Warm clothing, even in the summer; insect repellent and long sleeved clothing; picnic, binoculars, field guides, bathing suits if you plan to go to Pollett's Cove, optional.

**Time of Year**
Summer and fall.

**Precautions**
Stay away from the edge of the cliffs; leave enough daylight to return to your car.

**Facilities**
Stores in Pleasant Bay.

**Special Features**
Gampo Abbey, a Buddhist monastery, is close by but I suggest you don't disturb the monks. If you have a particular interest in the Abbey, you might want to write ahead and ask permission to visit.

Many of the beaches in northern Cape Breton are wild and beautiful, but not really suited for swimming. The rocky coast and unpredictable seas make some areas along the northern shores much more agreeable—in fact, totally awesome—for beachcombing and hiking. But you will find too some opportunities for invigorating and magical swims here and there, in protected bays, sheltered coves, or lakes.

The Information Centres at the entrance to the Cape Breton Highlands National Park (at Cheticamp and Ingonish) will give you details on the beaches within the park, like North Bay Beach and Black Brook. And here are two more you may want to try either for a swim, a picnic, a hike, a family outing, or all of the above.

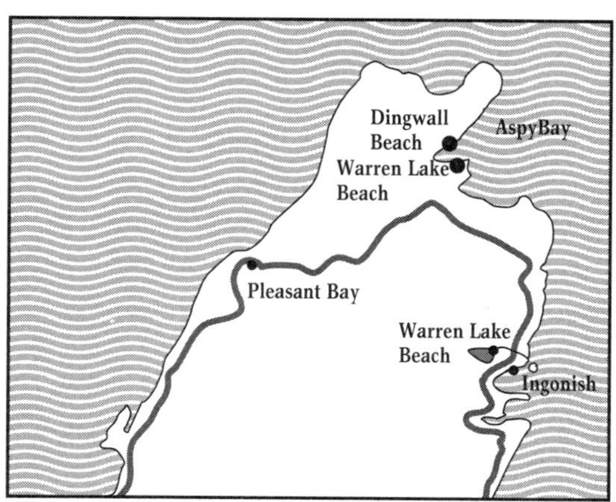


## DINGWALL BEACH

The beach at Dingwall is a glorious stretch of northern seacoast that looks the Atlantic straight in the eye. It's a fascinating mixture of ivory sand and white gypsum "cliffs," the gypsum being responsible for the white road on which you travelled to get there. A walk north along the beach will take you to a channel. On the other side is the tip of the beach at Aspy Bay. (See page 37 for more on Aspy Bay.)

**DIRECTIONS**

Take the Cabot Trail north through Ingonish and Neil's Harbour and turn off at the road to Dingwall, just south of Cape North. Drive down The Dingwall Road for 2 km (1.2 mi) until you come to Mountain View Road on your left. Turn there and drive a few hundred metres then turn right onto the road to the wharf. Hang left and you'll soon come to the white road on your left, leading over a small channel. Follow the white road to its end and park there.

## WARREN LAKE BEACH

This is an inland freshwater beach, located on Warren Lake just north of Ingonish on the Cabot Trail. It has excellent facilities for picnicking and swimming and there is also a beautiful woodland hiking trail around the lake. (page 159) It's a great family setting. Water is warm and beach is sandy.

**DIRECTIONS**

Take the Cabot Trail North from Ingonish, past the Broad Cove Campground, and turn left at the sign for Warren Lake. Drive in 2 km (1.2 mi) to the picnic site. Beach is to your left over a little footbridge and a short walk on a path through the woods.

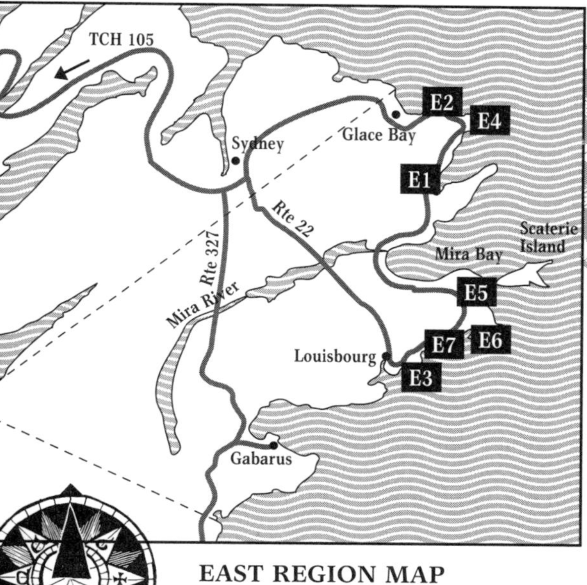


## EAST REGION MAP

**E1** Old French Mine Site, Port Morien

**E2** Fossil Hunting at Schooner Cove

**E3** Lighthouse Trail, A Walk through History

**E4** A Bird Walk Along Cape Perce

**E5** Coastal Hike - Main-a-Dieu

**E6** Coastal Hike - Baleine

**E7** Coastal Hike - Gooseberry Cove

E1

## OLD FRENCH MINE SITE, PORT MORIEN

***There are mines of coal through the whole extent of my concessions near the seacoast, of a quality equal to the Scotch, ... and also in France where I have brought them for trials.***

—Nicholas Denys, Paris, 1672

If you were to turn left at the old chowder house in Port Morien, and walk past the ballfield and down the path to the grassy shore of Cow Bay, you'd be standing on one of the most historic spots in North America.

Tucked away between the headlands of Cape Perce to the north, and South Head, this cozy little cove looks like just another bit of superb Cape Breton scenery and worthy of a visit for that reason alone. But the rich history of Cow Bay, and in particular this spot, offers visitors another dimension of enjoyment, and a walk along this shore without knowing its history would be a bit like a trip to the Bird Islands without binoculars.

The Mi'kmaqs called the bay *Noolektooch* ("place jammed with ice"). Later, according to a map in the Archives in Paris dated 1580, the French called it Baie de Mordienne, and it is probable that the shore of Mordienne was a seasonal habitation for Portuguese, Basque, and Breton fishermen.

By the early 1700s coal mining at Baie de Mordienne was becoming an important activity for the French in the New World who were building their magnificent fortress at Louisbourg, a little farther along the coast.

### A WALK THROUGH HISTORY

Perhaps the best way to get a feel for the comings and goings of eighteenth century Baie de Mordienne, is to take a walk along the path of history. This path leads you down over a grassy slope to the shores of Cow Bay (as it's now called), along the cliff for a short distance and then back up through the field to the road. It takes you from the early 1700s when commercial coal mining began here, to the late 1800s when Blockhouse Colliery was silenced forever.

### THE VERY FIRST MINE

As you walk down the path you'll approach the water's edge on the south side of the field. There on your right you'll see a deep indentation in the shoreline that slopes down to a flat rock ledge. It doesn't look like much now, but you're standing on the spot where in 1720 the first commercial mine in North America was dug. (see map pp 64)

*At the entrance to the Old French Mine.*

The French drove a tunnel into the coal seam from this point, twelve feet wide by half a mile long (3.7 m by .9 km). The coal was dug by hand, hauled to the wharf, and loaded onto waiting ships.

With the English on the prowl and much at stake, the French decided, in 1725, to build a fortification on the mine site to keep their miners, and their interests, safe. On the cliff, just above the mine, a fortification was built, with barracks and stores for the lodging of workmen, and a blockhouse—a tower-like structure with openings around the top for keeping watch and firing weapons.

If you were standing there overlooking the ocean on a typical working day in 1720, you could probably watch the Acadian miners hauling the coal from the pithead in carts that bumped and rattled their way down to the wharf. The double-masted ketches waited there to take their precious black cargo around the coast to Louisbourg. And in the blockhouse above you, a guard—possibly a soldier borrowed from the fortress—would be keeping a watchful eye for uninvited guests from land and sea.

## BLOCKHOUSE MINE CHANGES HANDS

For the next twenty-five years the French worked the mine, until the fortress at Louisbourg fell into British hands. For much the same reasons as the French, the British kept soldiers busy digging the coal. Four years later the French regained Louisbourg and returned to Baie de Mordienne to pick up where they had left off. According to a census taken in 1752, sixty-four people—all Acadians—lived at Mordienne.

## THE 1800s

Let's jump ahead now a hundred years or so. Fortress Louisbourg is long gone (destroyed once and for all by the British), the mine has been idle, except for bootlegging, for some time, and the buildings have disappeared from the field. The bay is now called Cow Bay, having been given the name sometime in the 1700s in honour of a cow that apparently strayed there.

It's 1852, and after many years of wrangling over ownership and licences, the site is granted to a Gaelic speaking Scottish Highlander named Hugh MacDonald. He sinks a new shaft near the blockhouse that breaks into the old French workings.

So begins another lively chapter in the history of the "blockhouse mine."

**THE BELLONIS**

In 1863 the Belloni family of New York bought the site and formed the Blockhouse Mining Company. Large-scale mining operations began. If you follow the path that leads down to the water's edge a hundred metres (109 yards) from the original French workings (The path was once the rail bed for the boxcars that hauled the coal), you'll see a small part of the original stone structure of the mine (see map pp 64).

Back up on the hill, try to picture what it might have looked like in 1866, with a workforce of four hundred men and boys working under and above ground. In the field, where you can now see a cluster of alders and small trees, three rows of company houses stood. What a different sight you would have seen then—the miners and their wives and children, going about their daily lives.

Pick up the path again that leads around the shore and back up behind the cluster of trees where the company houses were. Just

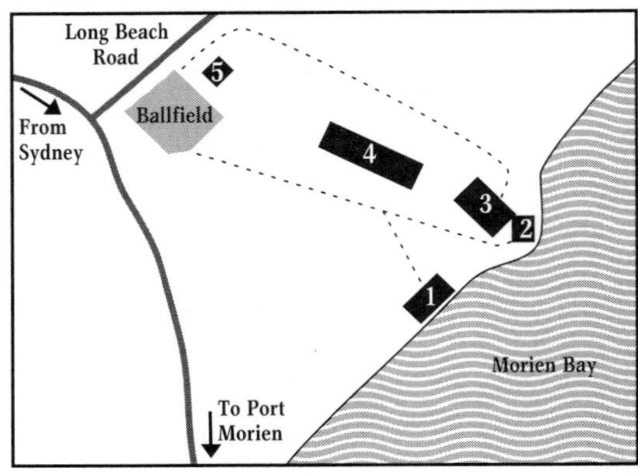


## Port Morien Mine Site

1 Old French Mine Site, 1720.
2 Site of Blockhouse Fortification, built in 1725.
3 Remains of Blockhouse Mine 1852.
4 Site of Company houses in 1866.
5 Site of Belloni Mansion, built in 1860s.

before you get back to the playing field you'll pass the site of the Belloni house (see map pp 64)—apparently a grand New York inspired mansion built by the family during prosperous times, but abandoned and left to the elements when hard times hit. Nothing remains of it now, not even a photograph.

By the late 1800s, after a valiant effort to keep their interests alive, the Belloni family gave up and went back to New York. In 1888, the Blockhouse Colliery, after more than a century and a half of notable success, coughed up its last ton of coal.

**DIRECTIONS**

Take the Sydney–Glace Bay Highway to the Donkin–Port Morien turnoff. Turn right and drive 4 km (2.5 mi) to the intersection at

Pachendale. Turn right again and drive 5 km (3 mi) to the Petro Canada service station. Turn right and drive 5 km (3 mi) to Port Morien playing field. Turn left onto Long Beach Road, and park by the field, and walk along the fence to your right. The path is between the backstop and the second set of bleachers.

PORT MORIEN • QUICK REFERENCE

**Activity**
A short stroll along a grassy headland where the first coal mine in North America was located in 1720.

**For Whom?**
Anyone.

**Conditions and Terrain**
Short, easy walk on grassy path, along Cow Bay and back along a woodland path.

**Distances**
Port Morien is about 20 km (12.4 mi) from Sydney; walk is about 1.5 km (1 mi).

**Time Required**
An hour or more. You may want to walk along the beach there too.

**Best Time of Year**
Summer and fall.

E2

# FOSSIL HUNTING AT SCHOONER COVE

How would you like to hold in your hand a piece of Cape Breton history that is, say, three hundred million years old? Sounds pretty far-fetched—unless you happen to be the type to go fossil-hunting along a Cape Breton beach.

If you're on the right beach and you know what to look for, the idea isn't as strange as it sounds. The beaches and coal fields of Cape Breton embrace some of the best fossil-bearing rocks in North America. There's a very good chance that you'll come across the remains of an organism that lived and breathed one hundred million years before the dinosaur.

Let's put that into perspective a little.

Back in the Coal Age—between 280 and 350 million years ago, when the earth's coal was formed—Cape Breton was a tropical, swampy land covered in huge ferns and trees. Over the years the swamps became filled in with mud and sand, and much of the lush vegetation eventually turned into peat—and, after a very long time, to coal. That's why Cape Breton is so rich in coal deposits and fossils.

One of the best fossil-hunting grounds for amateur hunters is the beach at Schooner Cove on the outskirts of Donkin. It's flat, safe for children, and easy to reach.

## GETTING STARTED

Before you actually hit the beach, though, there are a few things you should do: First of all, resist the urge to buy a knapsack full of fancy tools or rock-hounding equipment. Leave that to the professionals; do, however, scare up a good pair of hiking boots, a small hammer, and a chisel of some sort. Eye protection is essential for anyone who plans to break rocks. Even sunglasses are better than nothing.

If you would like to get some idea of what to look for, you might want to drop into the University College of Cape Breton Library. On the second floor there's a collection of Cape Breton fossils on display that will astound you. From the many specimens of ferns, tree bark, and roots, you'll get a pretty good idea of what lies waiting for you to discover.

**ON THE BEACH**

When you arrive at Schooner Cove, park your car just above the shore.

So there you are, standing on the brink of discovery, hammer and chisel poised for adventure. What now? How do you know which rocks are harbouring a three-hundred-million-year-old tree? Well, you don't. At least not on your first expedition. Just look for rocks that seem to be made of of layers—which is just about all of them. Those most likely to contain intact fossils are ones that have recently fallen to the beach from the rapidly eroding cliffs, or those that have been washed ashore by the tide.

A couple of light taps with the hammer and chisel will reveal any treasures that lie within. Keep in mind that fossil fields like this one are a very important link to our past. Once the fossils are gone, that link is broken forever. It is important to note that under the Special Places Protection Act it is against the law in Nova Scotia to dig fossils or artifacts without a permit. You can, however, "pick"

## Schooner Cove

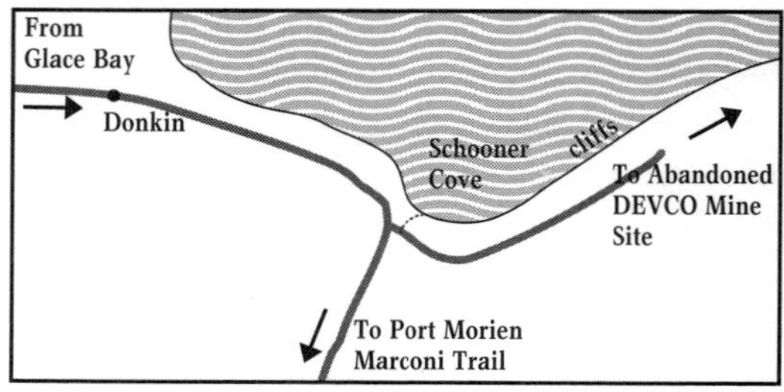


fossils that are loose, that is, not attached to the solid bedrock. Take only one or two fossils and be careful not to damage the beach. Confine your "hunt" to fallen rocks and those below the high-water mark since any fossils in these rocks will eventually be destroyed by the elements anyway.

As for what is actually there for you to discover, it's quite simple, at least for the amateur's purposes. Most of the fossils found here are one of two types—ferns or trees. You may find a seed pod or a cone from these plants as well, but they are not plentiful. There is the outside chance too that you could uncover a fossilized animal or fish, or maybe even a large insect, but this would be a rare find. If you do come across anything that looks bony, take it to the university, just in case.

Whether you find that fantastic rare specimen, or just an ordinary tree branch, or nothing at all, you'll find "digging up" the past a great way to spend a sunny Cape Breton afternoon.

### DIRECTIONS

From Sydney, take the Sydney–Glace Bay Highway (You'll find the university along this route, too) to the Donkin–Port Morien turnoff (about 12 km [7.4 mi]). Turn right and drive 4 km (2.5 mi) to the intersection at Pachendale. Turn right and drive 10 more km (6.2 mi)—keeping to your left all the way—to the village of Donkin. Just past the village you'll see a gravel road to your left, out along the water. Turn there and immediately take another left turn into a parking area.

SCHOONER COVE • QUICK REFERENCE

**Activity**
Looking for fossils on a beach.

**For Whom?**
A family activity.

**Conditions and Terrain**
The beach is easily accessible and rocks on the beach are flat and easily negotiated.

**Distances**
Donkin is about 25 km (15.5 mi) from Sydney.

**Time Reguired**
Allow at least two hours, or you can spend the whole afternoon.

**What to Wear/Bring**
Walking shoes or sneakers, eye protection, hammer and chisel.

**Time of Year**
Summer and fall.

**Precautions**
Hunt at low tide. Don't climb on cliffs or allow children to play under them. Take only one or two fossils.

**Note:** If you find a fossil, wash it gently with water; don't scrub or handle it any more than necessary, and never varnish it.

E3

# LIGHTHOUSE TRAIL: A WALK THROUGH HISTORY

***Since the 16th century, Louisbourg harbour has been a haven for mariners—Spanish, Portugese, English, French....***

—J. Johnston, "Canada's First Lighthouse,"

*Atlantic Advocate,* Feb. 1986.

In 1977 a group of university students, under the direction of staff at the Fortress of Louisbourg, undertook a study of the coastal area that runs from Lighthouse Point in Louisbourg to Little Lorraine, a community about 5.5 km (3.4 mi) along the coast to the north. Their purpose—to design a groomed hiking trail equipped with footbridges, boardwalks, parking lot, and washrooms, "so that all visitors to the park may more fully enjoy the natural history and beauty of the countryside."

*Lighthouse at Louisbourg.*

It was a wonderful idea. But it was not to be.

The two-volume proposal is still gathering dust on a library shelf, and the realization of the dream will have to wait for more prosperous times.

In the meantime, though, the coast of Louisbourg welcomes all who wander there, and the elements that inspired those young people back in 1977 are still very much alive and well today.

**THE TRAIL**

As you can see on the map, the northeast trail begins at Lighthouse Point on the north side of Louisbourg Harbour, just across from the fortress. It runs north along the coast, over barrens and rocks, through bogs and woodlands, to Little Lorraine. There's so much to say about this coast, it's difficult to know where to start. There's the human history that began several hundred years ago and the natural history that goes back five hundred million years, give or take a few million. There's the wildlife, the bird life, the flora, and the geology.

Let's begin at the beginning—with a little geology.

Most of the rock along this trail is of volcanic origin. It belong to the Fourchu Group dating back to the Pre-Cambrian Age—about six hundred million years old. It is some of the oldest rock in the world! For you rock hounds, this rock formation is made up mostly of tuffs and breccia, which are formed from rock spit out by a volcano during an eruption. You can spot also, sandwiched between layers of the dark green volcanic rock, strips of yellowish or light green lava rock, as well as reddish coloured quartz veins.

## HUMAN HISTORY

Before you start out on your walk (The trail begins just below the parking lot), stop and ponder for a minute a bit of the history of Lighthouse Point. When the French ship *Le Profond* almost ran aground in Louisbourg Harbour in 1727, the urgent need for a light became apparent. In 1733 the first lighthouse in Canada was built on the spot where you stand. It was 21.3 m (70 ft) high and could be seen 28.9 km (18 mi) out to sea on a clear day. Illuminated by fish oil and a circle of thirty-one cotton wicks in a bronze basin, the original light was, unfortunately, not fireproof and was destroyed by fire. Two more lighthouses were built on that site, and in 1922 the present light was erected and until a few years ago was operated by hand.

## THE BRITISH CONNECTION

The most turbulent and fascinating period of history for this short stretch of coastline was probably during the time of the two British seiges on the fortress—from 1745 to 1758. The French lights had been burning for eleven years when the British decided Lighthouse Point would be a good spot from which to bombard Battery Island, which is strategically located at the mouth of the harbour. To set up their firing site, the British had to ship by schooner six eighteen-pound cannons and a mortar. (The eighteen pounds refers to the cannonballs not the cannons!) They slipped into the harbour just out of range of Battery Island and dropped anchor about 1.5 km (1 mi) up the coast from the point. What a sight they must have been, hoisting those cannons up the cliff and dragging them over the rocks and bogs to their firing spot, in the shadow of the King of France's own lighthouse. Their efforts paid off and Battery Island was put out of commission.

**PLANTS, BIRDS, AND WILDLIFE**

If you're not too engrossed in the history of Lighthouse Point, you'll discover that its ecology, like its history, is complex and exciting. The terrain is an intriguing mixture of bog, barren, seashore, and woodland, each with its

## Lighthouse Trail

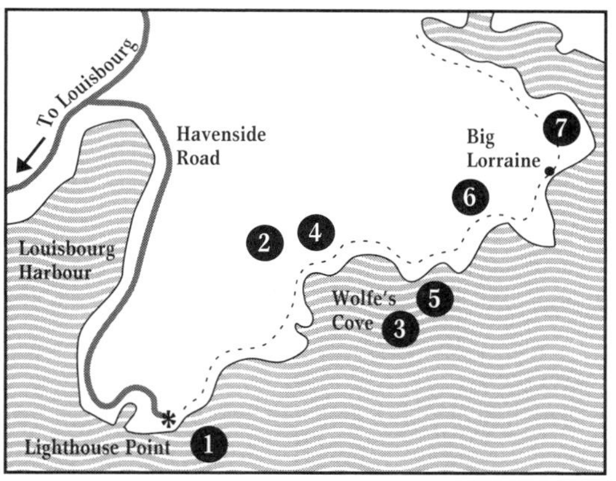


**1** Lighthouse Point - English fired cannons from here, 1745 and 1758.

**2** Foundation of 18th century fort.

**3** Wolfe's Cove where English landed their cannons and dragged them to Lighthouse Point.

**4** Possible site of old Mi'kmaq village.

**5** Hammerhead.

**6** A treasure was said to have been dug up here in 1900 or so.

**7** An Irish immigrant ship, the *Astrea,* ran aground in the early 1800s. Five hundred perished and only two survived.

own brand of vegetation. Hundreds of plants thrive here, in spite of the elements—rocky soil, salt spray, high winds, and chilly summers. You'll notice the misshapen evergreens bending inward, away from the sea, and the absence of any tall plants and bushes in the bogs and on the barrens. You'll be amazed, as I always am, by the colours, the textures, and the smells that surround you.

And, if you keep a sharp eye, you may spot flapping or gliding overhead a bald eagle, a marsh hawk, or any number of terns and sparrows. You might spot too, scooting along the edge of the wood, a red fox, a white-tailed deer, or a snowshoe rabbit or two.

Whatever your interests—history, botany, geology, or all three—I guarantee that one walk along Lighthouse Trail will not be enough. You'll want to go back again and again.

**DIRECTIONS**

From Sydney take the Louisbourg Highway (Highway 22) to Louisbourg. Just inside the town limits, past the S & L Railway Museum, turn left onto Havenside Road. This narrow, winding, very scenic road will take you directly to Lighthouse Point. Park your car in the space provided near the lighthouse site.

**Activity**
A walk along the coast of Louisbourg Harbour beginning at the site of oldest lighthouse in Canada; nature hike.

**For Whom?**
Not suitable for very small children, the elderly, or anyone with trouble walking.

**Conditions and Terrain**
Walking can be difficult at times over rocks where path has worn away. It can be foggy and cool along this coast even when it's hot elsewhere. Terrain is a mixture of bog, barren, woodland, and rocky shore.

**Time Required**
The entire trail will take five or six hours, but you can walk as long as you want and turn back.

**Distances**
Louisbourg is 37 km (22.9 mi) from Sydney; trail is 12 km (7.4 mi) return.

**What to Wear/Bring**
Good walking shoes, warm clothing, sunscreen. Field guides, picnic, and binoculars optional.

**Precautions**
Watch the path along cliff—parts have been eroded and are not safe to walk on. Watch for hidden holes in the bog and barrens—they can be quite deep. Protect yourself against the sun. Even when it's cool, it can burn.

**Special Features**
History, geology, wildlife, and flora are all fascinating. The Fortress of Louisbourg is across the harbour.

**Facilities**
Restaurants, stores, etc., in town of Louisbourg.

E4

# A BIRD WALK ALONG CAPE PERCE

You don't have to be a seasoned bird-watcher to enjoy an afternoon walk along a woodland trail hoping to catch a glimpse of a brown creeper or a nesting bobolink. And even though you may not know a thrush from a sparrow, that's no reason to let the "experts" have all the fun.

One of the best places in Cape Breton to watch birds is on a trail just east of the village of Donkin. There's a headland there called Cape Perce that takes you through three richly distinct bird habitats offering a golden opportunity to spy on some of North America's most sought-after woodland, marsh, and shore birds.

## FIRST STOP—THE MARSH

Just east of Donkin, on the Marconi Trail, an unpaved road leads off to the left past a small inlet known as Schooner Cove. Just beyond the cove, on your right, is a sprawling salt marsh that laps lazily around the cattails and alders. This is the home of one of the finest array of ducks and marsh birds on the island.

Park your car along the road and walk carefully through the thick grass. Find a spot to sit and listen. You'll probably only hear the whisper of the breeze through the cattails, or a few crickets passing the time of day. What you won't hear are the birds—not right away. They'll be silent for awhile, calculating the danger, watching. If you stay quiet, they will eventually show themselves. Then it'll be your turn to watch.

On the next page are three you will be likely to spot.

**Bobolink** (six to eight inches). Breeding male is mostly black with beige (or yellowish) streaks and pointed tail; beige patch on back of head; very distinct white patches where tail and wings meet body. Female is olive coloured, streaked with dark brown. In nesting season (June) the male is very noisy, and flies low over the nest, which is well hidden in the grass.

**Common Snipe** (ten to eleven inches). Upper body is mottled brown; white belly and beige breast; very long narrow straight bill; flight is fast and erratic. On breeding ground it performs a spectacular territorial display, making an eerie whistling sound as wind rushes through its feathers.

**Green-Winged Teal** (twelve to fifteen inches). Male's head and upper neck are chestnut coloured; very distinct glossy green patch from eyes to back of head. Back and sides are brownish-grey with black cross lines. In flight wings show a beautiful bright green patch, edged with cinnamon, white, and black. Female is similar but darker brown, and has no green patch around the eyes.

You could spend hours here, lulled by the sweet sounds and smells of the marsh, and the longer you linger, the more reason you will find to stay. But save some for another day. The rest of the trail awaits you.

**UPHILL AND INTO THE WOODS**

Drive a little farther up the road until you come to the end and the fenced-in site of the abandoned Donkin coal mine. Park to the left of the gate and take the path that leads uphill along the fence.

Don't be discouraged if at first you can't sort out the muddle of indistinguishable sights and sounds here. When I took my first bird hike with local "birder" Cathy Murrant, she stopped me every now and then and whispered things like: "Shhh, listen, there's a boreal chickadee" or "Look over there, it's a Savannah sparrow!" I finally had to confess to her that I not only didn't see what she was pointing at, I hadn't even heard anything distinguishable. Her advice: try to tune in to one voice at a time, then follow the sound with my binoculars. It worked. I soon caught on.

As you walk uphill along the path, you head into a dense woodland area. What intrigues me is how much the smells and sounds differ from the marsh. The air is cooler and carries with it a potpourri of juniper and balsam, seaweed and peat moss. And, of course, the clear solos—distinguishable-with-a-little-practice—of the woodland birds have replaced the harmonious pandemonium of the marsh.

Focus your binoculars, tune in your ear, and see if you can spot these woodland residents:

**Brown Creeper** (about five inches). Brown, streaked with white and beige, long pointed tail, long curved bill. Feeds by working its way up and around the tree, digging for insects, and, after it reaches a certain height, flying to the base of another tree and starting again. Has a soft lisping call as it feeds; nests in spring under loose pieces of bark on dead trees.

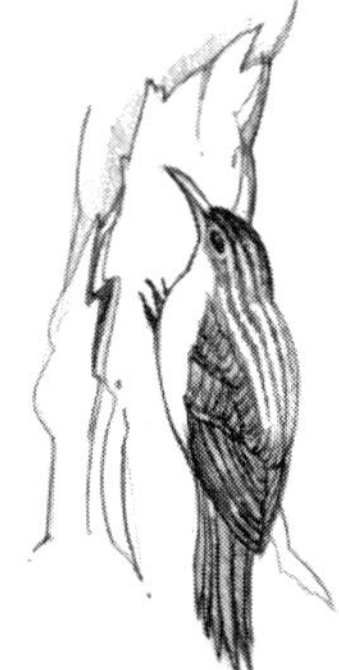

**Yellow-Shafted Flicker** (twelve inches). This is a woodpecker. The male is grey with a red band on the back of its neck; back is grey-brown with broken black lines; light brown face with black "moustache"; underside of tail and wings is bright yellow; wide black band under throat; female has same markings but no "moustache." Loud repeated flickering sound is its call.

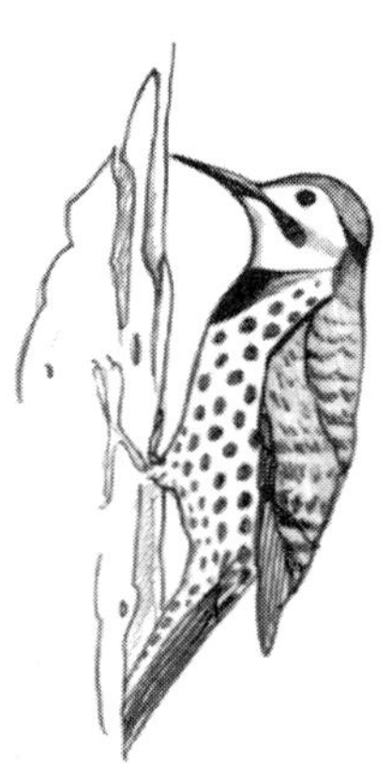

**Boreal Chickadee** (about five inches). Crown and back are brown, throat is black, and cheeks are white; has reddish-brown sides and white underparts. Its "chick-a-dee-dee" sound is nasal and slower than that of other chickadees.

**OUT TO THE HEADLAND**

Once you come out of the woods, you'll find yourself high on a headland looking out to sea. On a clear day you can see the light on Flint Island straight ahead. Beneath you the shale cliffs drop almost perpendicularly to the shore. The berry-laden barrens spread around you like an endless Persian carpet, and the breeze is pure Atlantic.

Follow the path along the headland toward the point. Be sure to stay on the path; the cliffs are dangerous. What may look like a solid foothold along the edge may be nothing more than a precarious overhang of loose earth and moss that could give way even under the weight of a child. Besides, there's so much to see out here on the headland that you'll want to focus all your attention on what's happening around you. If there's no fog you can see Scatarie Island to the east, and during lobster season you can look below you onto the decks of the boats and watch the fishermen hauling their traps.

And, of course, the birds! Keep your eyes on the fields, the cliffs, the sky, and the sea. Here are two to watch for:

**Greater Yellow Legs** (about fourteen inches). A slender grey-streaked wading bird with bright yellow long legs, a white breast spotted with black, and a darkish back; its call—a distinct whistling sound—will alert you to its whereabouts. Sometimes they wade in the water up to their belly.

**Kittiwake** (sixteen to eighteen inches). The highlight of your trip will be the kittiwake. These are small gulls not commonly seen by mainland observers. They winter far out to sea and usually nest on offshore islands; the colony here on the cliffs of the cape is an exception. Nests are perched on cliffside on small ledges. You'll probably hear the birds before you see them. Bird lovers consider it a real treat to be able to observe these noisy little sea birds so closely. Adults are white with pale grey back and wings; very noticeable black tip on wing; feet are black, bill is yellow.

The birds mentioned here are only a small sample of those you might see on your walk along Cape Perce. A field guide will help you identify others and Cathy Murrant of Port Morien will be happy to share her knowledge. Give her a call at 737-2684. If you would prefer a guided tour, ask Cathy about that too.

# Cape Perce

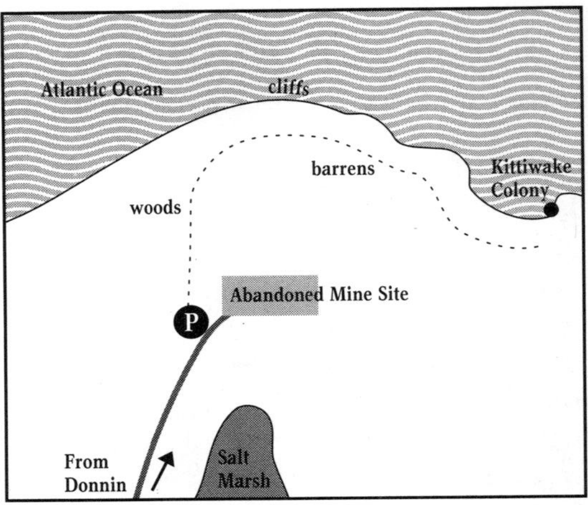


**DIRECTIONS**

From Sydney take the Glace Bay Highway to the Donkin–Port Morien turnoff (about 12 km [7.4 mi]). Turn right and drive 4 km (2.5 mi) to the intersection at Pachendale. Turn right and drive 10 more km (6.2 mi), keeping to the left all the way, through the village of Donkin. Just past the village there's a gravel road to the left. Turn there and drive a short distance until you see the salt marsh on your right.

**Activity**
A walk along a headland to spy on some of the many marsh, woodland, and sea birds that make their home there.

**For Whom?**
Not recommended for the very young or the elderly.

**Conditions and Terrain**
A fairly easy walk but uphill partway. The path is easy to follow over the barrens of the headland.

**Distance**
Donkin is about 25 km (15.5 mi) from Sydney. The walk along the headland is 3 to 4 km (1.9 to 2.5 mi) return.

**Time**
Allow two to three hours at least.

**What to Wear/Bring**
Walking shoes, binoculars; warm clothing; picnic, field guides optional.

**Time of Year**
You'll find birds there any time of year. The ones mentioned will be seen mainly in spring and summer.

**Precautions**
Stay well back from the edge of the cliff. The ground is unstable and dangerous. Never disturb nesting birds.

# THREE COASTAL HIKES: MAIN-A-DIEU, BALEINE, AND GOOSEBERRY COVE

Like three sisters born with distinctly different personalities, Main-a-Dieu, Baleine, and Gooseberry Cove are related by their location on the southeast coast of Cape Breton, but each possesses its own special character. A walk along the seacoast at any one of these craggy locations reveals Cape Breton at its starkest (at its best, some say), and will turn up treasures on each shore that you may not find anywhere else on the island.

---

*Go beachcombing—you're sure to find something of interest.*

## MAIN-A-DIEU

E5

Main-a-Dieu is the most northerly of the three communities. A drive through the village is reason enough to go there. Like most fishing villages along that shore, Main-a-Dieu looks every bit the part: houses clustered around the harbour, looking seaward; brightly coloured fishing boats swaying side by side along the wharf; the barrenness of the landscape; the dominance of the sea.

But if you want to truly tune in to the wonders of Main-a-Dieu, don't be satisfied with a drive through town. Take a walk around Moque Head. The coastline there is a pure

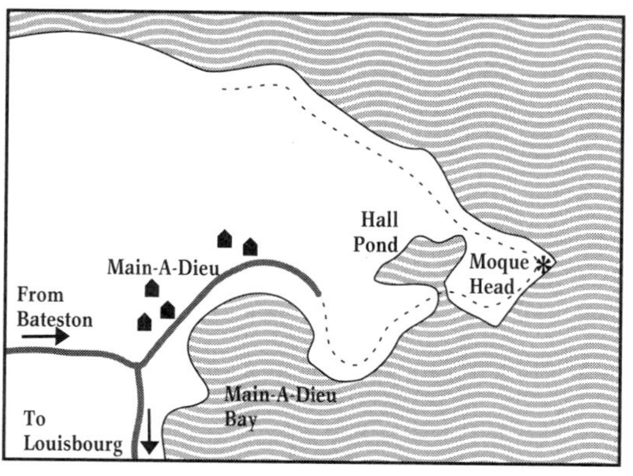


**Main-A-Dieu**

Atlantic mix of rocky shore and woodland, bog and barren. The plant life will astound you: labrador tea, beach pea, Solomon's seal, wood sorrel, cranberries, crowberries, and cloudberries—to name just a few. And the smell of balsam fir, creeping juniper, wintergreen, and salt sea air will fill your nostrils like some exotic smouldering incense.

The trail from Main-a-Dieu around Moque Head begins on the hill overlooking the village. Park your car there and follow the path that leads you northward, around the coast and out to a beach. When you get to the beach you'll have to cross a narrow channel that's usually filled with water—but it isn't deep. Boots come in handy here, but bare feet and rolled-up pants will do the trick.

Once across, keep a sharp eye out for the path, which you'll find on the ocean side of the power line, through a narrow opening in the evergreens. (There's a tree stump next to the opening, but don't count on it as a permanent landmark.) Walk carefully uphill through the trees a short piece until you pick up the path. From here the path is easily followed out to the grassy cliff of Moque Head overlooking Main-a-Dieu Passage. You'll stand next to Moque Head foghorn (if it's a foggy day you'll get to hear it!) and ahead of you Scatarie Island and its lighthouse rise out of the ocean.

From there continue on the path—watch for spots where erosion is forcing the path perilously close to the edge—until you come to another glorious beach. Behind you is Hall Pond and beyond that, even though you may think you've left them far behind, are the houses of Main-a-Dieu. You can continue along through an intriguing field of sun-bleached tree stumps and up along Mira Bay, but I would suggest that you turn back when the trail begins to deteriorate into an animal track.

**DIRECTIONS**

Take the Louisbourg Highway (Highway 22) from Sydney to the turnoff to Main-a-Dieu (25 km [15.5 mi]). Drive to the yellow light at

Bateston (5 km [3 mi]), keep right and drive 7 km (4.3 mi) to Main-a-Dieu. Turn left at the intersection and follow the road through the village and up the hill. Park on top of the hill. The path leads down from the parking spot.

**SPECIAL FEATURES**
View of Scatarie Island lighthouse; a picnic park and beach in the village.

**FACILITIES**
Stores in the village.

**Note:** You will find the path occasionally separating into two branches at the beginning of the trail, but they converge after a short distance.

## BALEINE

**E6**

A little south of Main-a-Dieu, the community of Baleine lies all but deserted except for the occasional house and the sea birds. A remote location, the most easterly point of "mainland" Cape Breton, Baleine's history goes back well over three hundred years to a time when it became the first settlement on the Island.

The village still has an air of intrigue about it. I had no trouble imagining it as being a perfect haven for seafaring pioneers. As you walk over the boggy headland and along the ragged coast, the view of the Fortress of Louisbourg to the south will help conjure up images of the days when men and women from faraway countries built their homes, and their lives, here on these shores.

One of my most memorable images of Baleine, though, is of the present rather than the past. As my family and I walked for the first time over the beach leading to the headland, we encountered a group of people walking back carrying buckets. The buckets were filled with what looked to me to be unripe blackberries. They weren't blackberries, they were cloudberries (or "bakeapples," as many people call them) and there on the beach, from perfect strangers, I not only learned where to find them, but how to preserve them, how to cook them, and where to find more. It was the first time I'd heard of the bakeapple.

## Baleine

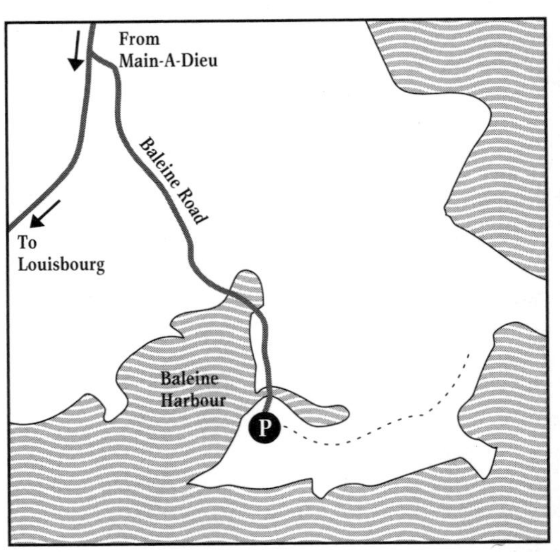


### THE TRAIL

The walk along the headland begins at the beach, where you park your car and head north towards Main-a-Dieu. You can, in fact, walk all the way to Main-a-Dieu, but it's a 14 km (8.7 mi) hike along some pretty rugged terrain. If you are so inclined, you may want to consider taking two cars and leaving one at the beach in Main-a-Dieu. If you would prefer just a leisurely afternoon hike along one of the most appealing and fascinating coasts on the island, then pack a little lunch, cross the beach at Baleine, and take a stroll along the headland. You'll be glad you did.

**DIRECTIONS**

Take the Louisbourg Highway (Highway 22) from Sydney to the Main-a-Dieu turnoff. Drive 5 km (3 mi) to the yellow light. Keep right and drive 7 more km (4.3 mi) to Main-a-Dieu. At Main-a-Dieu turn right and drive 4 km (2.5 mi) to the Baleine turnoff, then 2 km (1.2 mi) down the Baleine Road to the beach.

**SPECIAL FEATURES**

View of Fortress of Louisbourg across the bay.

## GOOSEBERRY COVE E7

Gooseberry Cove is another one of those gems along the southeast shore of Cape Breton that has much to offer the curious wanderer. No matter how often I return there, I make new and exciting discoveries with each visit.

I'm not sure how Gooseberry Cove got its name, since I've never found gooseberries there. What I have found, though, on my many afternoons wandering there, is just about everything else—blueberries, cranberries, foxberries, juniper berries, cloudberries, partridge berries, and crowberries. They've all found a home in the bogs and barrens. And two of my favourite wild plants grow abundantly—the blue flag iris, dwarfed and brilliant from the sea air, and the intriguing insect-catching pitcher plant, almost indistin-

*Spend an afternoon berry picking along the bogs and barrens of Gooseberry Cove.*

guishable among the reds and greens of the coastal terrain.

You can spend your day on the beach, or walk the path over the sometimes boggy, sometimes rocky shore. Unless we've had an extended dry spell, a walk along the path will almost certainly be wet going, so wear boots. I was surprised at the amount of water those bogs can hold. I'm told it's a matter of geology. The grass and soggy earth underfoot is really just a shallow layer of earth covering a cliff of rock. When it rains, the rock won't absorb the rain, so it stays on top and its only escape is to evaporate, which in the damp, often foggy climate of the Atlantic coast, isn't as easy as it sounds.

## DIRECTIONS

Take the Louisbourg Highway (Highway 22) from Sydney until you come to a small sign to Lorraine on the right-hand side of the road. Directly across from the sign is a road—don't

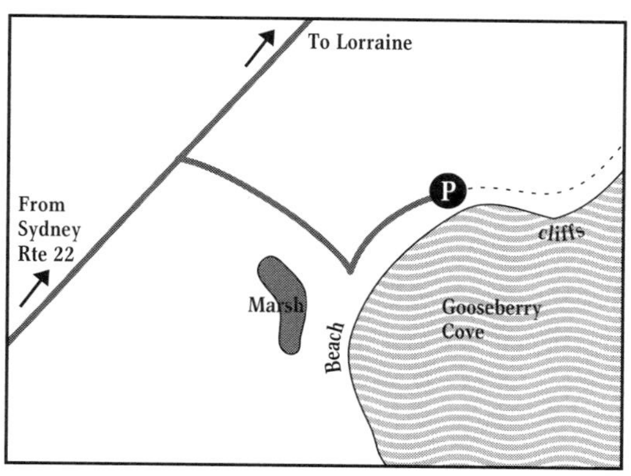


**Gooseberry Cove**

take it; take the next left. Drive 5.5 km (3.4 mi) until you see a narrow road with a gate. Pass that road and watch carefully for another narrow road a very short distance further along—it's partly hidden by alders. Turn in there.

## SPECIAL FEATURES

Incredible coastal barrens and bog, wild plants, and flowers.

**Activity**
Three walks along the south coast of the island.

**For Whom?**
Not recommended for small children or the elderly.

**Conditions and Terrain**
All three locations are a combination of rocky shore, barrens, and bog. Paths are not always clearly defined and you will almost certainly encounter some wet spots.

**Distances**
All three paths go on for several kilometres. The longest walk is from Baleine to Main-a-Dieu.

**What to Wear/Bring**
Boots come in handy as bogs are wet. Take warm clothing even in summer. Wind from the ocean can be cold and fog can roll in quickly.

**Time of Year**
Summer and fall.

**Precautions**
Watch for hidden holes in the bog and barrens —they can be deep. It's best to stay on the paths.

Many people are familiar with the eastern shore of Cape Breton because the Fortress of Louisbourg, with its fascinating history, is located there. It's a coast with many inlets and bays, headlands and barrens, stories and legends. And many wonderful beaches.

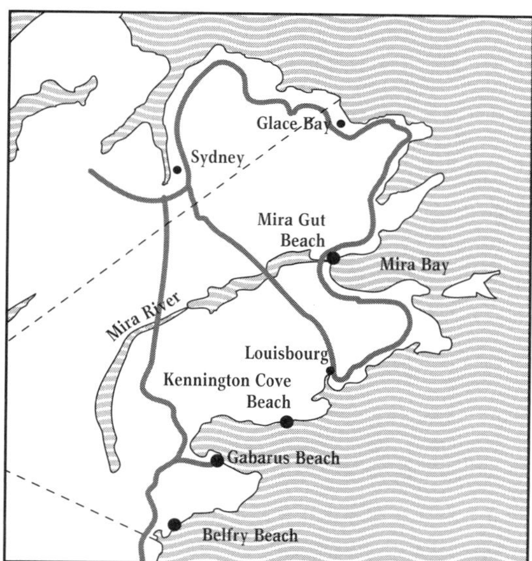


## KENNINGTON COVE

Kennington Cove is a glorious sandy beach, flanked by grassy hills and white-capped sea. Angelica (thought to have been brought by the French in the 1700s) grows there in great profusion, and you'll find up the little brook from the shore a deep pool of fresh mountain water—too enticing not to take a dip in.

As you lie on the beach, walk along the hills, or refresh yourself in the mountain pool, you might want to contemplate a little of the cove's fascinating history. Here, in June of 1758, shiploads of British soldiers and sailors came ashore and set up camp along the cove.

Some 27,000 men were landed in this enormous military operation. By travelling overland through the woods, they attacked the Fortress of Louisbourg, eventually defeating the French and taking possession of the fortress.

*Kennington Cove is a glorious sandy beach.*

**DIRECTIONS**

Kennington Cove is about 20 km (12.4 mi) south of the Fortress of Louisbourg. Without directions, it can be tricky to find. Take Highway 22 (Louisbourg Highway) south from Sydney to the town of Louisbourg. Drive through town until you come to the monument and the Park Administration sign. Turn right and drive (pavement ends after about 1 km [.62 mi]) to another Park Administration sign. Turn left there and drive straight to the intersection. You'll see the fortress in the distance. Turn right and drive from there until you come to the beach and picnic site (about 24 km [14.9 mi] in all from the town).

## MIRA GUT BEACH

This beach is located at the mouth of the Mira River where it empties into Mira Bay. It's a great family beach with lots of sand and a very gradual slope into the water. Keep away from the far (south) side of the breakwater, as there is an undertow. Because Mira Gut is easily accessible from Glace Bay, Sydney, and other centres, it's very well used during July and August.

**DIRECTIONS**

Take the Louisbourg Highway (Highway 22) south to Hornes Road. Turn left and drive 10 km (6.2 mi) to an intersection. Turn right. Park your car along the road.

## GABARUS BEACH

The road to Gabarus will take you right to the seawall that runs the length of the beach. It's an amazing stone and wooden structure built, I presume, to protect the small village from the sea, which is literally on its doorstep. It provides protection too for the fleet of fishing boats snuggled into the cove. The grey sandy beach is typical of south shore beaches, and is protected somewhat by two headlands—Rouse Point and Rams Head. You can walk along the beach, or along the seawall itself.

If you're up for a more challenging walk, give Gull Cove a try. Take the road that runs to the east of the village (a right turn where the Gabarus road meets the seawall) and drive (or walk) about 1 km (.62 mi) to a cemetery. Park there and follow the trail. It's a 10 to 12 km (6.2 to 7.4 mi) hike return if you go all the way to the end. You'll walk through woodlands and along coastal barrens and eventually arrive at the site of an old fishing village. There are still some remnants of foundations left.

### DIRECTIONS

From Sydney take Exit 7 off Highway 125 (the Bypass) onto Route 327 south to Marion Bridge (14 km [8.7 mi] to bridge). Cross the bridge and drive about another 3/4 km (.46 mi) to the turnoff to Gabarus. Watch for the sign. Turn left there and drive 20 km (12.4 mi) to an intersection. Turn left to Gabarus. Drive to the end of the road.

## BELFRY BEACH

As you can see on the map, Belfry Beach is situated on a very narrow strip of land that separates Belfry Lake from Fourchu Bay. It's an incredibly beautiful spot with the lake behind you, the ocean in front of you, barrens and fields and sand as far as the eye can see. I've been told you can walk this beach all the way to Gabarus. I haven't tried it—yet! There's a channel running from the lake to the ocean that at high tide is a great place for children to swim, and there are ever so many walking opportunities around the lake, along the beach or over the fields.

### DIRECTIONS

From Sydney take Exit 7 off Highway 125 (the Bypass) onto Route 327 south to Marion Bridge (14 km [8.7 mi] to the bridge). Cross the bridge and drive 3/4 km (.46 mi) to the turnoff to Gabarus. Watch for the sign. Turn left there and drive 20 km (12.4 mi) to an intersection. Turn right towards Fourchu and Framboise and drive about 10 km (6.2 mi) until you see a small sign for Belfry Road. Turn left and drive down that road to the end (about 1 km [.62 mi]). Just before you get to the beach, there's a road to the left that will take you a little farther up the beach to the channel that flows from the lake.

SOUTH REGION

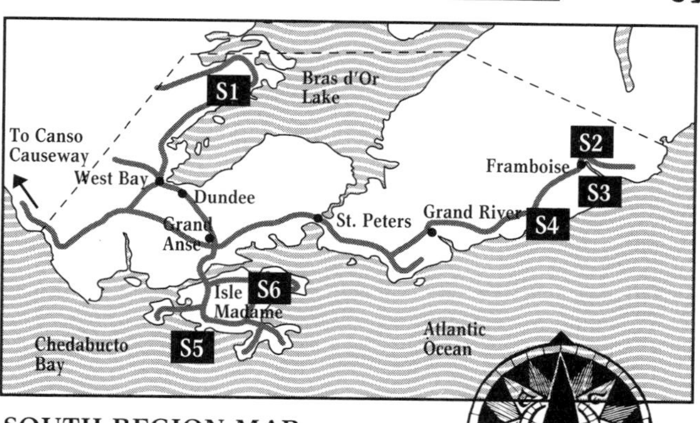


## SOUTH REGION MAP

- **S1** A Day at Marble Mountain
- **S2** Digging Clams at Fuller's Bridge
- **S3** Overnight Camping at Framboise
- **S4** Hike to Fox Cove near Framboise
- **S5** Walk Around Crichton Island
- **S6** A Road Tour of Isle Madame

S1

# A DAY AT MARBLE MOUNTAIN

***I see a marble quarry. Its walls rise sheer above the village—a majestic ruin... no sound of busy work is heard.... Here then is the explanation of the ruined and deserted houses of the village.***

—Clara Dennis, *Cape Breton Over,* 1942

There's something about Marble Mountain! I'm not sure if it's the breathtaking view out across Bras d'or Lake from the top of the quarry, or the glorious beach glistening with white marble sand. Or maybe it's just the ghosts of a resplendent past, still lingering.

Whatever it is that keeps me going back, one thing's for sure—it's a very special place. All that's left of the community now is a handful of houses dotting the once-flourishing hillside, a museum that stands guard over memories of better days, and a mountain of white marble partially eaten away by a long-gone prosperity.

## A LITTLE HISTORY

Actually, it wasn't all that long ago that the mountain reeled with the comings and goings of a thriving industry. Nicholas Brown, a geologist from Prince Edward Island, accidentally discovered the marble seam in 1868. (He had come to Cape Breton looking for oysters!) By the early 1900s, Marble Mountain was booming. It was home to well over a thousand people and the quarry employed 750 men.

The squeaking pulleys and conveyor belts no longer carry the gleaming white chunks across the road and down the cliff to the waiting barges. And the descendents of the workers have long since left the place, "gone down" the road to better days. But as I drive through Marble Mountain, I find it easy to picture a time when the beach was littered with the steel trestles and smokestacks of industry, and on the road above, rows of company houses buzzed with the activities of a turn-of-the-century working class existence.

*MacLaughlin's Store, Marble Mountain, in 1908.*

*MacLaughlin's Store today.*

## FIRST, THE BEACH

Tucked away as it is in the maze of mountains and tiny communities that surround West Bay, Marble Mountain isn't the sort of place you're likely to pass through on your way anywhere. But if you're willing to veer a little off the beaten path, it will be well worth your effort. On a sun-drenched August day, the beach alone is reason enough to take a side trip there. Apart from the quarry—and the memories—the beach is probably Marble Mountain's only legacy of its commercial heyday. The crushed marble sand still glistens like opals in the sun, and a swim there is, and always will be, pure magic.

You'll have to watch carefully for the road to the beach. There's a footpath just across the road from the quarry, but it's very steep and unsuitable for older persons and small children. The road will be much more to most people's liking. Driving into the community from West Bay you will pass two churches on the left. Just past the churches is a large house on the right that was once a general store. Take the road that runs beside that house (It looks more like a driveway) and follow it downhill, past the wharf, to the beach. Park anywhere along there.

## FROM THE BEACH TO THE MOUNTAIN

As you make your way along the beach, you'll notice the remains of a trestle that once supported conveyor belts carrying the blocks of prized marble down from the quarry, across the road, and onto the barges. If you look up, you can see the mountain, and the abandoned quarry. A climb to the top of the quarry is a singular adventure, and if the

*Looking out over the Bras d'Or from the top of the quarry.*

climb itself doesn't take your breath away, the view out over the bay surely will!

To get to the quarry from the beach, drive back up the beach road and turn right (east) onto the main road. Less than a kilometre (.62 mi) will take you to the picnic area on your right and a road, blocked by a gate, leading uphill on your left. Park your car at the picnic site and walk across the road and up the hill. About two-thirds of the way up, before you reach the quarry, you'll come to a small clearing to your right and a path that leads up the edge of the quarry. Follow the path, but take your time. It's steep!

Once you're at the top, let yourself slip back for a minute to the days when the quarry below rang with the clacking of horses hooves as boxcars rattled over steel rails that fanned out from the giant crusher in the centre like so many spokes on a great cartwheel.

You can almost smell the smouldering hardwood from the limestone kiln hundreds of feet below on the beach. And out in the bay, the tiny silent islands, with names like Calf Island and Cow Island, can still conjure up memories of days when farming families worked the soil and cattle grazed in the fields.

However you spend your day at Marble Mountain, I think you'll discover, as many before you have, that in spite of its sleepy serenity, or perhaps because of it, it's a place and a feeling that will stay with you long after the white mountain and the glorious beach fade slowly behind you in your rear-view mirror.

## Marble Mountain

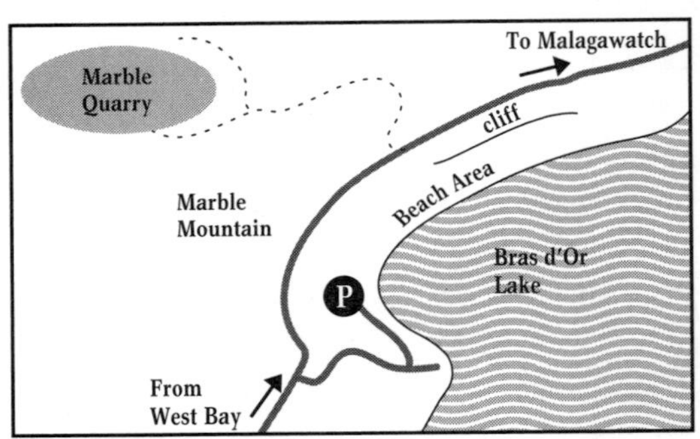


**DIRECTIONS**

Drive to Grand Anse, 17 km (10.5 mi) west of St. Peters, on Route 4. At Grand Anse take the turnoff to Dundee. Drive 10 km (6.2 mi) to Dundee and at the intersection turn left to West Bay. Drive 6 more km (3.7 mi) to a stop sign; keep right and drive 18 km (11.1 mi) along the bay to Marble Mountain.

**Activity**
Swim, picnic, hike to top of quarry; historical site.

**For Whom?**
Beach is accessible by car for anyone. The hike up the quarry is very steep and not suitable for the very young, the elderly, or anyone with problems walking.

**Conditions and Terrain**
The beach is quite large with lots of white marble sand. The trail is steep but easy to follow.

**Distances**
Marble Mountain is about 34 km (21 mi) from the turnoff at Grand Anse; the hiking trail up the quarry is less than a kilometre (.62 mi) long.

**Time Required**
A few hours, but you can easily spend all day.

**What to Wear/Bring**
Bathing suit, towels in summer; insect repellent; sunscreen; picnic, binoculars, field guides optional.

**Time of Year**
Summer and early fall.

**Precautions**
Pace yourself on the way up the quarry trail and don't let children run on the way down.

**Facilities**
There are no stores in Marble Mountain. The nearest one is in West Bay.

**Special Features**
Marble beach; magnificent view from top of quarry; interesting history. Small museum is open in summer months. Home of novelist Margaret MacPhail, who wrote her first novel *Lock Bras d'Or,* when she was in her eighties. An American entrepreneur has chosen Marble Mountain as the ideal site for his winery, complete with vineyards—coming soon!

S2

## DIGGING CLAMS AT FULLER'S BRIDGE

If you would go to almost any length for a feed of really fresh seafood, you should consider a clam-digging excursion to Fuller's Bridge. Fuller's Bridge is on the south shore of Cape Breton, just west of the Richmond County line. There's a river there that empties into the sea, and at low tide it transforms into a maze of grassy channels and mud flats—some of the best clam-digging territory on the island.

*Clam digging—a fun way to enjoy the low tide. All you need is a bucket and a small shovel.*

One of the great things about clam-digging is that it doesn't require any special talent, preparation, or equipment. All you need is a bucket, something to dig with (preferably, but not necessarily, a pitchfork), boots or old sneakers—and, of course, a very low tide!

## THE TIDE

Ideally, you should arrive at Fuller's Bridge about a half hour before the tide is dead low. After about an hour and a half you will see the tide beginning to rise again. Stay another half hour or so, then call it a day. The channels fill up quickly, so don't stay too long. You don't want to be stranded on a mud flat, in the middle of a river, with the tide coming in.

## THE CLAMS

As for knowing where to dig, don't worry—the clams will show you. While they're down under munching away on whatever it is clams munch on, they shoot water from their shells to get rid of unpalatable particles. This makes little holes in the sand. If there's a hole, there's usually a clam. If you spot a bunch of holes, you've hit pay dirt. Dig in!

Anything sharp will do: a pitchfork, a small shovel, or even a gardening tool. Dig back a bit from the holes to avoid breaking the shells, and be careful picking them up—they have sharp edges!

## SIGHTS AND SOUNDS

You might want to stop your digging every now and then to look around and to listen. The bird life here is almost mesmerizing. The last time I was there, two mother ducks paddled nonchalantly on a nearby pond with their broods, and herons watched a little suspiciously from a distant sandbar. Snipes sprinted over the mud flats around me and some flapped overhead. Gulls patiently circled, waiting for a free lunch. When they all piped down a bit, I could hear the slapping of the ocean against the rocks, just beyond the trees.

## BACK TO THE CLAMS

You won't find a lot of really large clams here. Three to four inches is about average. Any smaller than that, rebury in the mud. Any broken clams can be left on the surface for the opportunistic birds circling overhead. Rinse the "keepers" off and check for "duds." A "dud" is a clamshell filled with sand. It can ruin your whole day if one gets into the cooking pot. A live clam will have its "snout" protruding from the shell, so it's easy to spot a fake.

And don't forget to keep your eye on the tide!

## FEASTING

When you get home, or to your campsite, rinse the clams and cover them with cold tap water. Throw in a handful of rolled oats or a couple of tablespoons of vinegar—it's not absolutely necessary, but it helps the clams to spit out the sand. Leave them for two hours, or as long as overnight.

When you're ready to feast, rinse them again, and put them into a pot with an onion, a celery stalk, and a clove of garlic (all optional, but definitely desirable), and just enough water to cover the bottom of the pot. The water in their shells comes out while the clams are cooking. Cover and let them steam for about fifteen minutes, or until the shells open. If any shells don't open, throw them away. If you don't happen to have a pot, wrap the clams in several layers of foil—no need for water—and toss them on the barbecue.

Spread some newspapers on the picnic table, dump the steaming clams into the centre and dig in. You won't need a pitchfork for this!

# Fuller's Bridge

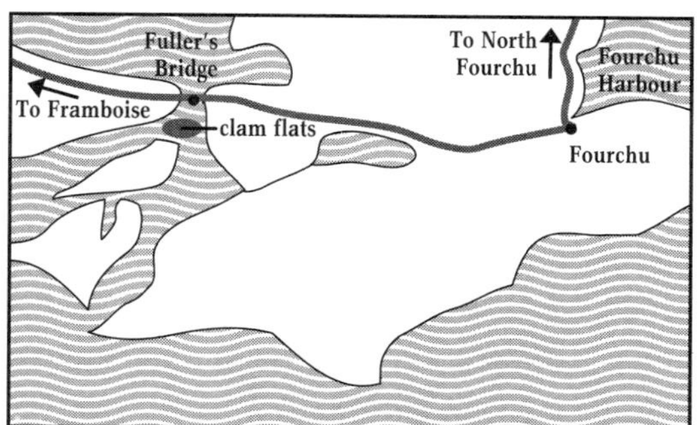


**DIRECTIONS**

From Sydney take Exit 7 off Highway 125 (the Bypass) onto Route 327 south to Marion Bridge (14 km [8.7 mi] to bridge). Cross the bridge and drive approximately 3/4 km (.46 mi) to the turnoff to Gabarus. Watch for the sign! Turn left there and drive 20 km (12.4 mi) to an intersection. Turn right towards Fourchu. After 22 km (13.6 mi) you'll come to an intersection (just after you drive through the village of Fourchu). Turn right toward Framboise and drive 2 km (1.2 mi) to Fuller's Bridge.

FULLER'S BRIDGE • QUICK REFERENCE

**Activity**
Digging clams in mud flats.

**For Whom?**
A good family outing but not suitable for very small children.

**What to Wear/Bring**
Wear high boots or old sneakers (keep dry ones in car); digging tool (pitchfork, shovel, gardening tool); bucket; gardening gloves, field guides, binoculars optional.

**Time of Year**
Early summer to late fall.

**Distance**
Fuller's Bridge is about 58 km (36 mi) from Sydney.

**Precautions**
Channels are soft-bottomed and can be deep. Watch children carefully; watch hands when digging (shells are sharp); watch tides. Don't stay too long. For tide times call Environment Canada, Sydney (564-7299) or listen to CBC Information Morning from 6 A.M. to 9 A.M. weekdays.

**Facilities**
Store in Fourchu or Framboise.

**Note:** Dept. of Fisheries officials say clams at Fuller's Bridge are safe to eat anytime because ocean tides keep water cold. However, if we have had a very long, hot spell, you may want to check it out yourself. (Sydney: 564-7700 during office hours.)

# OVERNIGHT CAMPING AT FRAMBOISE



If you're the type of camper who wouldn't think of pitching a tent anywhere but under a security light, next to the washroom, in a supervised campground, you probably won't enjoy camping at Framboise.

On the other hand, if you're the type who would love to set up camp beside a beautiful wilderness lake just where it narrows and runs off into the ocean, and wake at dawn to the doleful cry of a loon, then Marie Joseph Lake in Framboise may be the place for you. There's a spot there, just where the lake empties into the Atlantic, that provides one of the most inspiring backdrops for a camping expedition you're likely to find anywhere.

You can camp right on the shore of the lake, fish or swim, pick berries or watch birds for the afternoon, explore the beach, and fall asleep to the rhythm of the ocean's everlasting surf. When I camped there with my family, a loon on the mist-covered lake woke us not long after dawn. As as we rekindled our campfire for breakfast, we could hear the occasional "plop, plop" of fish (salmon and trout, so I'm told) breaking the surface of the still water in search of their own breakfast.

After breakfast, when the fog drifted reluctantly back out to sea and the fields and woods yawned to life, we packed up a snack, grabbed our fishing rods, and headed over the brook and up the hill to Fox Cove (see page 114). We felt a little like the Swiss Family Robinson.

## FINDING THE SPOT

Just west of the general store in Framboise, a

very short distance from where the pavement meets the gravel road, you'll see a sign to Crooked Lake. Drive down this road until you come out of the wooded area and begin to see open fields. On your right is a narrow road alongside a field. Drive down this road—slowly, it's not in good shape—for about 1 km (.62 mi) to the beach. On your left is the Atlantic and on your right is Marie Joseph Lake. You'll know you've found your campsite when you see a small cluster of stunted evergreens, the remains of other campers' campfires, and the site's one and only modern convenience—a garbage can, complete with lid.

## CAMP WITH CARE

This seems like a good place to say a little about conservation.

This incredible piece of land is privately owned. Permission has been given for overnight camping on the condition that campers follow a few basic rules in order to protect the ecology of the area.

The first rule is to pitch your tent on the spot—near the cluster of little evergreens—where others have camped before you. This limits any effect on the area to that one spot. Next, if you build a fire, use the fire ring. And keep it small. For kindling and firewood (if you haven't brought your own) use driftwood from the beach. Never cut live trees. Or better still, buy some wood from the local general store. Use the garbage can that's been provided, but never leave your garbage behind. Take it away with you! Try your best to leave no sign at all that you were even there.

Other campers who come after you will appreciate it. The landowner will appreciate it. And the plants and creatures around you, most of which you won't even see, will appreciate it.

## Framboise

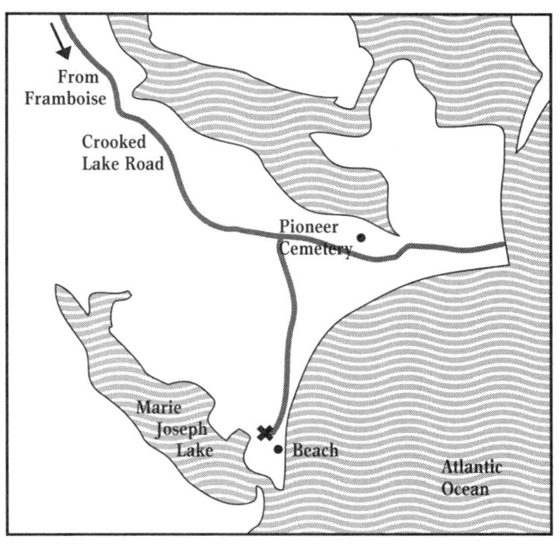


**DIRECTIONS**

From Sydney take Exit 7 off Highway 125 (the Bypass) onto Route 327 south to Marion Bridge (14 km [8.7 mi] to the bridge). Cross the bridge and drive about another kilometre to the turnoff to Gabarus. Watch for the sign. Turn left there and drive 20 km (12.4 mi) to an intersection. Turn right towards Fourchu. After 22 km (13.6 mi) you'll come to an intersection (just after you drive through the village of Fourchu). Turn right toward Framboise and drive until you pass the general store in Framboise. Just beyond that is the end of the pavement and the Crooked Lake Road.

**Activity**

Overnight camping expedition with no facilities; nature and coastal hike.

**For Whom?**

Not recommend for infants or very small children.

**Conditions and Terrain**

Camp site is very close to the open Atlantic, so expect fog, especially in the evening and early morning. It's usually colder on the coast than inland. There's a good surface for tent and some protection from the ocean breezes; lake in front, beach behind; fields and woods all around.

**Best Time of Year**

Summer or early fall.

*Pack a picnic lunch and spend the day exploring.*

**What to Wear/Bring**

Keep in mind that your car will be close at hand, so you won't have to walk any distance to your campsite. However, try to bring along just the necessities—tent, sleeping bags, pillows, dishes, cooking pots, dishcloths, utensils, camp stove (Unless you're a seasoned camper, cooking over a campfire can be pretty tricky), food (preferably in a cooler; homemade soup or stew is perfect), drinking water, first aid kit, insect repellent, sunscreen, garbage bags, lantern and/or flashlight, matches, newspapers (to help start fire), overnight clothing and toiletries, soap and towels, axe.

**Optional:** Air mattresses, fishing rods and bait, field guides, binoculars, TV (just kidding!).

**Precautions**

If you have a tarpaulin for your tent, take it! The fog can be quite pervasive during the night. Build only small fires and watch them carefully. Check forest fire index before you go. Take warm clothing and bedding. Watch children in lake and near the ocean surf, (there can be undertows). Don't disturb nesting birds.

**Facilities**

The general store in Framboise has pretty well anything you may have forgotten.

**Special Features**

Wildlife, plants, flowers, shells, mushrooms, and berries galore. There are apparently lots of fish in Marie Joseph Lake and Fox Lake.

S4

# HIKE TO FOX COVE NEAR FRAMBOISE

One of the things that amazed me most about the delightful hike along the south shore of Cape Breton is the lavishness of the wildflowers, plants, mushrooms and fungi, berries, birds, and just about anything else that grows. Exposed as these fields and headlands are—swept by salt spray and often fierce ocean winds, not to mention shrouded in fog a good part of the time—I expected to find barrens and rocks and not much else. I couldn't have been more wrong.

In fact, I think I have never seen as many varieties of growing things in any other area. My first visit there was in August and here is just a sample of what my family and I came across on that short path to Fox Cove. We saw many varieties of mushrooms and fungi, such as boletus, fly agaric (poisonous), and chanterelles; strawberries, blueberries, foxberries, cranberries (not quite ripe), raspberries, blackberries, cloudberries, and crowberries; blue flag iris, wood sorel, lambkill, purple fringed orchis, meadowsweet, one-flowered Wintergreen and Canadian burnett. And that was just on the ground. On the lake the loons called, overhead shorebirds glided, and from his perch on the branch of a tree in a clearing a bald eagle watched as we passed.

## THE TRAIL

Park your car in the clearing beside Marie Joseph Lake and look for a spot in the channel that you can cross easily. You may have to wade knee deep, depending on the time of year and recent rainfall. Once on the other side, walk along the beach then up the hill along the path. The path follows the headland high above the shore. It's only about 1.5 km (.9 mi) to Fox Cove. There's a glorious beach there and a still water that runs off into the ocean. If you remembered your fishing rod, you may have some luck in the still water. It looks like a great place for trout.

If you want to walk further, the path continues up through the woods (You'll have to look around a bit for it) and along another grassy headland.

So dig out your fishing rods, don't forget the picnic and field guides, and put them all to good use along the shore to Fox Cove.

## A VISIT TO A PIONEER CEMETERY

When you get back to Marie Joseph Lake and drive back up the beach road, instead of turning left onto the Crooked Lake Road to get you back to the highway, turn right and drive a short piece down towards the water. You'll see a sign to a pioneer cemetery on the left. The cemetery is on a little windswept hill overlooking the bay.

If you're inclined to enjoy poking around headstones, you'll find the epitaphs here conjure up a time when life was fragile and dangerous, not only for men who battled the sea, but also for women who bore children under dangerous circumstances and children who were susceptible to the many diseases from which death was the only escape.

## DIRECTIONS

From Sydney take Exit 7 off Highway 125 (the Bypass) onto Route 327 south to Marion Bridge (14 km [8.7 mi] to bridge). Cross the bridge and drive another 3/4 km (.46 mi) or so

## Fox Cove

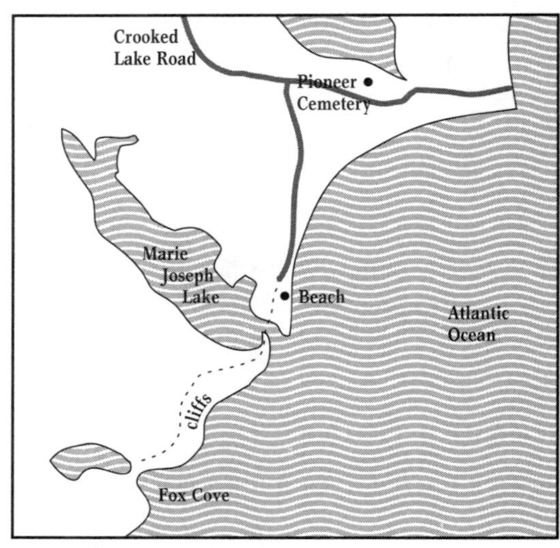


to the turnoff to Gabarus. Watch for the sign! Turn left there and drive 20 km (12.4 mi) to an intersection. Turn right towards Fourchu. After 22 km (13.6 mi) you'll come to an intersection (just after you drive through the village of Fourchu). Turn right towards Framboise and drive until you come to the general store in Framboise. Just past the store is the end of the pavement and the Crooked Lake Road. Drive down Crooked Lake Road until you come out of the woods and begin to see open fields. On your right is a narrow road alongside a field. Drive down that road—slowly, it's not in good shape—until you come to the beach. Park your car there and walk across the channel to the other side. The path to Fox Cove is just up the beach and over the hill.

**Activity**

Coastal hike along Framboise Cove; fishing; picnic; visit to a pioneer cemetery.

**For Whom?**

Not recommended for the elderly or anyone with problems walking.

**Conditions and Terrain**

Hike is coastal, mostly over fields and barrens, and is a little hilly in spots. You must cross the channel at the beginning of the trail that is sometimes knee-deep, other times very shallow.

**Distances**

The hike to Fox Cove is about 3 to 4 km (.9 mi to 2.5 mi) return. The path continues beyond Fox Cove.

**Time Required**

One and a half to two hours.

**What to Wear/Bring**

Wear good walking shoes or sneakers; bring bathing suits and towels, insect repellent, sunscreen; field guides, fishing rods, bait, picnic optional.

**Precautions**

Watch children in ocean when there is a high surf—it can create an undertow. Marie Joseph Lake drops off close to shore. Stay back from the edge of the cliffs, they are unstable and dangerous.

**Special Features**

Wildlife and plants galore; shore and woodland birds; beautiful beaches and views of ocean; pioneer cemetery; lovely lake to swim in.

**Facilities**

There's a general store in Framboise just before you turn down the Crooked Lake Road.

S5

# A WALK AROUND CRICHTON ISLAND

Whenever I take a walk along the coast of Cape Breton, or a stroll along the shores of Bras d'Or Lake, I'm always intrigued by the many tiny islands that adorn our lakes and ocean, like beads on an Indian headdress. It's a rare lofty lookoff that doesn't reveal at least one offshore jewel—usually, alas, just a short boat ride out of the reach of those, like myself, without a boat.

*Watching the waves at Broad Cove.*

But there are a few small islands around that, for one reason or another, aren't entirely out of reach and whenever I come across one, I waste no time checking it out.

## THE ISLAND

Crichton Island, happily, is one of the accessible ones. Actually, it's an island off an island off an island. Lying just off the southwest coast of Isle Madame (which is just off the south coast of Cape Breton), Crichton Island wasn't always walker-friendly. It wasn't until a breakwater was built to protect fishing boats in the harbour at West Arichat that you could walk to the island. I suspect that the breakwater was once also crossable by car, but today, because of years of exposure to the ocean's fury, only foot traffic is tolerated by the badly deteriorated structure. I have a feeling, too, that it won't be many more years before the sea reclaims its territory and sets Crichton Island free once again from its mainland moorings.

In the meantime, though, the island awaits, and the short walk across the breakwater will get you there safely, providing you heed the following two warnings. First, watch your step: the cement underfoot, although solid enough for walking, is badly gouged and cracked and requires some careful treading. Second, don't try to cross the breakwater when the sea is high. It was built to "break" the waves before they enter the harbour, so getting washed off is a real possibility. On a calm day the only connection you will feel with the sea, aside from experiencing its awesomeness all around you, is a gentle salt spray caressing your face.

## ONCE YOU GET THERE

The island is uninhabited, although it wasn't always so. As you approach its western side, you will see the remains of a farm—a very old orchard and the remnants of an outbuilding or two.

## THE TRAIL

Start your walk on the path that leads to your right from the breakwater and follow it along the shore and through the woods. If you keep on the path you will eventually come to a large field at the other end of the island and the navigation light. From there, you can retrace your steps back along the path or, if you're more adventurous, walk along the shore around the exposed side of the island. You can also cut across the island via one of the paths that lead off from the main path. A trip around the island is about 4.5 km (2.8 mi), either on the path or along the shore.

I was surprised to find here, on an island off the south coast of Cape Breton (one of the most rugged coastlines in North America), vegetation and wildlife such as I expected only to see in protected inland locations. The waters of Chedabucto Bay here on the west side of Isle Madame are much more forgiving than the open Atlantic on the eastern side at places like Sampson Cove and Rocky Bay.

When I visited Crichton Island in late summer, I found raspberries and blueberries galore, dozens of species of wildflowers—turtlehead, yellow loosestrife, white and purple fringed orchis—and shore and woodland birds. Fall brings foxberries and cranberries, and, no doubt, some wintering or migrating birds. And I'm told any time is a good time to spot seals on their way in and out of West Arichat Harbour.

The magnificent view from the island, across to West Arichat, is classic—the typically Acadian-looking houses along the shore; the yellow, red, and turquoise fishing boats bobbing in the harbour; the wharf, the gulls, and the church.

It all adds up to a liberating lift for landlocked spirits.

# Crichton Island

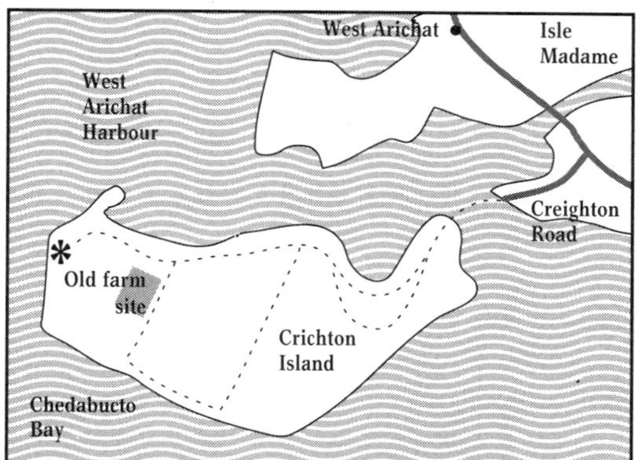


**DIRECTIONS**

Take Exit 46 to Louisdale off the Fleur de Lis Highway. Drive straight through the flashing yellow light, over the Lennox Passage Bridge. At the intersection of Route 206 and 320, turn right onto 206 south toward Arichat. At West Arichat (about 7 km [4.3 mi] from turnoff) just past the Co-Op Store, you'll see Creighton Road. Drive down this road and park by the breakwater.

**Activity**
A walk over a breakwater and around a small island.

**For Whom?**
Some parts of the walk are not suitable for small children or the elderly.

**Conditions and Terrain**
Walking is quite easy generally and the trail is well-defined. Near the end of the island where the light is located, the path goes into the woods and gets a little soggy. The beach is mostly rocky.

**Distances**
A walk to the end of the island and back is about 4.5 km (2.8 mi).

**Time Required**
About one and a half hours return on trail.

**What to Wear/Bring**
Walking shoes, long-sleeved and long-legged clothing; insect repellent; field guides, picnic optional.

**Time of Year**
Summer and fall.

**Precautions**
Blackflies can be bad in the woods on a still day so go prepared. Don't cross the breakwater when the sea is high. Watch children carefully on the breakwater at all times.

**Special Features**
Beautiful views of Isle Madame and ocean; lots of berries, wildflowers, birds, and sometimes seals.

**Facilities**
Nothing on island; store in West Arichat.

# A ROAD TOUR OF ISLE MADAME



If you're in the mood for a little exploring but can't quite muster the energy for a hike through the woods or a climb up a mountain, you might want to consider taking a driving tour around beautiful Isle Madame.

*Experience the Acadian flavour of Isle Madame.*

Isle Madame is a little-travelled rugged island on the southwest coast of Cape Breton peopled mostly by Acadians whose history goes back almost three hundred years. You can spend just a few hours there, or do what I did—pack a lunch and make a day of it. Even from your car as you pass through the tiny fishing settlements and occasional bustling town or village, you'll pick up the distinct Acadian flavour of the island. If you stop off now and then, as I did, at a museum or on a deserted beach, you'll discover more of what it was about Isle Madame that attracted those early settlers.

Although you can tour Isle Madame in either an easterly direction or from the west, if you're not familiar with the roads I suggest you follow my directions. Road signs are scarce and a few wrong turns could have you going in circles.

**WEST ARICHAT AND JANVRIN ISLAND**
At the intersection, just over the Lennox Passage Bridge, turn right onto Route 206. The drive through the woods here is short and you'll soon come to West Arichat and the coast. About 6 km (3.7 mi) from the intersection you'll come to the turnoff to Janvrin Island, your first detour off the beaten path.

Turn right and follow the road until you come to a sign to Janvrin Harbour. Turn right and drive along the water's edge, weaving in and out of the little coves and inlets that dot this scenic drive. You won't actually cross over to Janvrin Island until you've driven 5 or 6 km (3 to 3.7 mi), although you may have

*Take a lesson in blacksmithing at Le Noir Forge, Arichat.*

thought you were on the island long before that. A sign welcomes you. At Janvrin Harbour, about 1 km (.62 mi) from the sign, you'll find a road to the wharf, which takes you to the heart of the community. The road comes to an end a short distance beyond the wharf. It occurred to me as I drove along Janwin Island that it is a perfect place for a family bicycle hike. The roads are paved, little travelled, and flat. The scenery is fascinating through a car window; it must be much more so from the seat of a bicycle.

**BACK TO THE MAIN ROAD AND ON TO ARICHAT**

Retrace your route back to West Arichat and Route 206. Turn right onto Route 206 and continue on to Arichat, about 6 km (3.7 mi) down the road. Arichat is the largest community on Isle Madame and the county seat of Richmond County. Its history is rich, and the charm of its old buildings and its proximity to the sea will enchant you.

Drive through the village until you come to the courthouse on your left. To your right is a street that heads downhill towards the water. Turn onto the street, then take a left at the bottom. This is the Lower Road and here you'll find Le Noir Forge, a restored eighteenth-century blacksmith shop with a working forge, and a little further on, Turnstone Pottery, a working studio and craft shop. At the forge you'll get all the history you want and maybe even a little lesson in blacksmithing. At Turnstone Pottery, artist and potter Jack Ouellette welcomes visitors, and I think you'll find his unusual pottery a refreshing break from the ordinary.

## ON TO PETIT-DE-GRAT AND SAMPSON COVE/ LITTLE ANSE

From Arichat, your next stop is Petit-de-Grat (pronounced, if I may presume to anglicize it, "petty-de-graw"), just a few kilometres along that Lower Road. The name, it's believed, is a combination of French and Basque words meaning "a spot where cod is dried," so named by fishermen who are thought to have fished here as far back as the 1600s. If you stop here long enough to chat with some "Petty de-Grawers," you'll probably hear stories of smugglers and pirates and, of course, Gabriel Sampson, Petit-de-Grat's first permanent resident.

When you reach the church, cross the bridge then turn left at the Co-Op store. Follow the road up the hill to Sampson Cove and Little Anse. Just a short drive uphill, around—and around—a few coves, and out to the Atlantic will get you there. The drive along this narrow seaside road will delight you as you twist your way past the tiny houses that decorate the barren hillsides like brightly coloured balloons at a birthday party. The sea is a way of life here, and I predict you won't be able to resist stopping off for a more intimate glance—a walk along the beach or a picnic on the shore.

Find your way back to Petit-de-Grat—don't forget to turn right at the Co-Op store—cross the bridge and drive straight back through the community until you come to a turnoff. (Watch for the giant flower box; in summer, when it's overflowing with flowers, it's easy to spot.) Turn right.

## NORTH TO PONDVILLE AND ROCKY BAY/ CAP LA RONDE

Drive about 2 km (1.2 mi) from the turnoff,

then turn right again onto Route 320 north. As you can see from the map, you've changed direction now and are heading across the island to the north shore. You can go straight north to D'Escousse, or take a scenic detour, or two, to Pondville and/or Cap La Ronde.

About 5 km (3 mi) north on Route 320, you'll come to a spot where two roads run off to the right. The first road takes you to Pondville and out to a beautiful protected beach where you'll find picnic tables, a hiking trail, and washrooms (of the "outhouse" variety). A swim here on a warm sunny day would certainly refresh a road-weary traveller. The second road, parallel to the Pondville Road, will take you along the Bay of Rocks, through the community of Rocky Bay, to an intersection. A right turn there will take you 2 km (1.2 mi) to the end of the road and Cap La Ronde.

*Enjoy a stroll and a picnic at the Martinique Picnic Park, Isle Madame.*

## ALONG THE NORTH SHORE TO D'ESCOUSSE AND MARTINIQUE

Coming back from Cap La Ronde, drive straight through the intersection (Don't turn back onto the Rocky Bay road) and drive about 4 km (2.5 mi) to D'Escousse. The coast along the north shore is a wonderfully rugged pure Atlantic experience, and the drive along

Route 320 through Poulamon and Martinique will be a fitting finale to your day. At Martinique you'll find a historic provincial park where you can swim, picnic, or enjoy the air on one of its groomed walking trails.

**HOME AGAIN, HOME AGAIN**

From Martinique follow Route 320 until you come back to where you started—the intersection of Route 320 and 206. Drive straight through the intersection, over the bridges to the yellow flashing light. Straight through the yellow light will take you back to the ramp for the Fleur-de-lis Highway (either east or west). A right turn at the yellow light will take you to St. Peter's via the old road, through River Bourgeois.

## Isle Madame

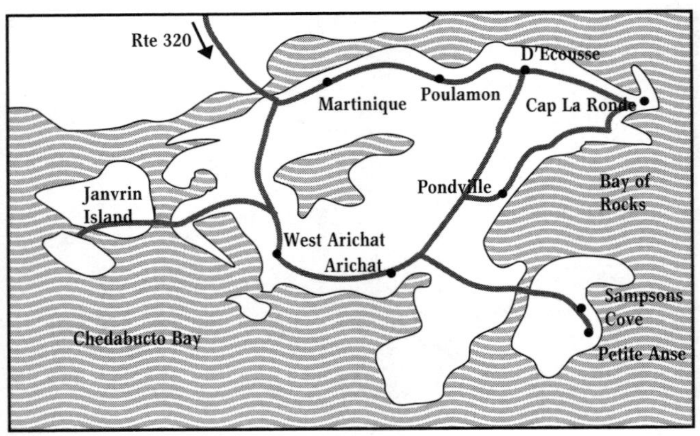


**DIRECTIONS**

Take exit 46 to Louisdale, off the Fleur-de-lis Highway. Drive straight through the flashing yellow light, over the Lennox Passage Bridge, to the intersection of Routes 206 and 320.

**Activity**
A driving tour around beautiful Isle Madame, with stops at historic sites, a pottery studio, and beaches.

**For Whom?**
Anyone.

**Time Required**
Give yourself at least three hours from the time you reach Isle Madame.

**Time of Year**
Spring, summer, and fall.

**Special Features**
The scenery is magnificent; historic site and pottery studio in Arichat, beautiful beaches.

**Facilities**
There are small stores in most communities and full services in Arichat.

ISLE MADAME • QUICK REFERENCE

The southern region of Cape Breton has many many beaches—from the sparkling warm waters of Dundee and Marble Mountain on Bras d'Or Lake, to the protected waters of the Strait of Canso, to the wide-open ocean shores of Pt. Michaud and Framboise. Take your pick, or try them all.

## PONDVILLE BEACH

The Pondville beach is a well-tended provincial site with toilet facilities and picnic tables. There's a channel running in behind the beach that forms a lovely pond, and you'll find a hiking trail there that overlooks the Bay of Rocks. The beach is sandy, and although the water is a tad cold, it is very clear and refreshing.

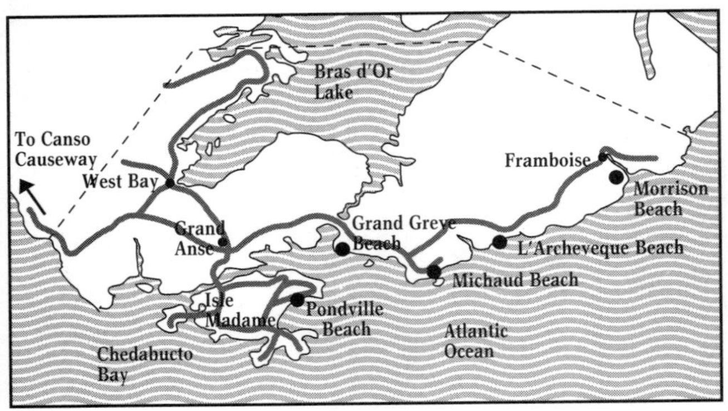


### DIRECTIONS

Take the Louisdale Exit off the Fleur de Lis Highway (which runs between Port Hawkesbury and St. Peters). Follow Route 320 around Isle Madame, through D'Escousse until you come to the Provincial Picnic Park sign and a road going to Pondville North. Alternatively, you can approach this turnoff by driving along the other side of the Island on Route 206 through Arichat and pick up Route 320 just past Arichat. The Pondville road is about 5 km (3 mi) from Arichat.

## GRAND GREVE BEACH

When you come down over the hill, just above this beach, past the little house with the white fence, the view of the beach will delight you. There are inlets and coves galore, a salt marsh with abundant flora and birds, and opportunities for hiking and exploring to please even the most sophisticated adventurer. The water you may find a little cool.

### DIRECTIONS

Just east of the town of St. Peters on Route 4, you'll come to a Department of Transport building. Turn there onto Route 247 (There's a sign there to Pt. Michaud, but it is difficult to spot). Drive down this road for 2 km (1.2 mi) until you come to a gravel road on your right and another easily overlooked sign that says "Grand Greve." Turn there and drive another 2 km (1.2 mi) or so to the beach.

## L'ARCHEVEQUE BEACH

L'Archeveque is a tiny fishing community tucked away in a cove on the south shore, not far from Grand River. The beach itself isn't one of the best for swimming—it's a little pebbly and fairly exposed—but it is a great spot for a picnic, a walk along the little headland, or a quick dip if the day is very hot. The wharf, fishing boats, colourful fish shacks and typical south coast charm provide a perfect backdrop for photographs.

You may want to stop off at Grand River, too, on your way. It's a wonderful little village at the mouth of the Grand River, renowned for its superb salmon fishing.

**DIRECTIONS**

At Soldier's Cove, about 10 km (6.2 mi) east of St. Peters on Route 4, take the road to Grand River. After driving about 10 km (6.2 mi) to Grand River, turn left onto the bridge and drive 9 or 10 km (5.6 to 6.2 mi) until you see the sign for L'Archeveque. Turn right and drive to the end of the road (about 1 km [.62 mi]). You can get to L'Archeveque from Framboise by continuing west past Framboise until you see the sign (about 25 km [15.5 mi] from Framboise). Directions to Framboise from Sydney are on page 115.

*Luxuriate in the solitude and the sun at one of the islands sandy beaches.*

## MORRISON BEACH

This is another one of the glorious south-shore beaches that seem to stretch into infinity. Like Belfry Beach, just up the coast, it is situated on a narrow strip of land with stillwaters on one side, ocean on the other, and a maze of grassy barrens and channels all around. For the explorer this is paradise. The swimming, as always on this shore, is invigorating. Be mindful of undertows if there is a high sea—this is open Atlantic.

### DIRECTIONS

From Sydney take Exit 7 off Highway 125 (the Bypass) onto Route 327 south to Marion Bridge (14 km [8.7 mi] to bridge). Cross the bridge and drive another 3/4 km (.46 mi) or so to the turnoff to Gabarus. Watch for the sign. Turn left there and drive 20 km (12.4 mi) to an intersection. Turn right towards Fourchu. After 22 km (13.6 mi) you'll come to an intersection (just after you drive through the village of Fourchu). Turn right towards Framboise and drive about 6 more km (3.7 mi) until you see a small sign for Morrison Beach. Turn left onto the gravel road and drive about 1 km (.62 mi) to the beach at the end of the road.

## PT. MICHAUD BEACH

Pt. Michaud Beach is one of the most spectacular beaches on the island. Its ivory sand stretches for miles around the shallow cove and out to the point. Children enjoy the long roll of the surf, and a hike along the beach to the point is an awesome experience.

**DIRECTIONS**

Just east of the Town of St. Peters on Route 4, you'll see a Department of Transport building. Turn there onto Route 247 (There's a sign there for Pt. Michaud, but it is difficult to spot). Drive down Route 247, through the village of L'Ardoise, until you see a Provincial Park sign. Keep a sharp eye for the sign; it's small. Turn at the sign, drive up the hill overlooking the beach, and park.

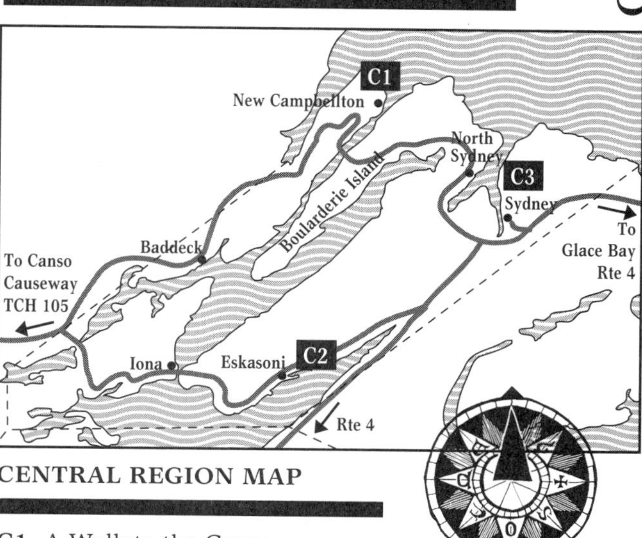


## CENTRAL REGION MAP

- **C1** A Walk to the Caves at Cape Dauphin
- **C2** Through the Brook to MacIntosh Falls
- **C3** History Walk Through Sydney's North End

C1

# A WALK TO THE CAVES AT CAPE DAUPHIN

I believe that the real heart and soul of a place like Cape Breton lies somewhere just beyond the well-worn tourist trails—down a country road or along a deserted beach. If that's true, it would make Cape Breton about ninety-nine percent heart and soul.

There's a trail on the New Cambellton Road, for instance, that is Cape Breton at its best. It's a woodland path that winds you gently around Kelly's Mountain, uphill along a brook, down a dry riverbed to explore a cave, and eventually out to the ocean.

## THE TRAIL

When you come to the end of the New Cambellton Road, park your car along the road and take the trail that follows the brook up into the woods. The path is not a well-groomed trail, and at times you'll have to walk around, under, or over a windfall. If you leave the path to walk around a fallen tree, be sure to pick up the path again on the other side.

After you've been walking for about forty-five minutes, you'll hear a soft rumbling, like thunder, in the distance. It's a brook that you have to cross. Depending on the time of year and recent rain fall, getting across won't slow you down too much. A few well-chosen rocks (watch it, they're slippery) should do it.

Not far from the brook you'll find yourself along the edge of a deep, dry riverbed. The path will lead you down the hill and into the gorge. Look across and make a mental note of where the trail leads up the far side of the bank. You'll want to continue on later, but first you should visit the cave.

## THE FOUR-HEADED MONSTER

Walk down the dry riverbed until you see a spot where a spring has found its way to the gorge and starts the river flowing again. Just to your right is the cave. Don't be afraid to go in—it opens up a little inside. The musty, mossy smell is enticing, and the "drip, drip" of the seeping springs adds an eerie feeling. When my seven-year-old crawled out from her first visit, I asked her what she saw. "Not much," she said, "just a four-headed monster who kept flushing the toilet."

Retrace your steps up the dry riverbed to the spot where you left the path and pick it up again on the other side. It gets a little steep and overgrown along this last part of the trail, but once you get to the clearing overlooking the ocean, you'll be glad you made the effort. The sensual, woodsy smell of the conifers is gone now, replaced by the salt sea spray. And the sweet sounds of the woodland birds can no longer be heard over the boisterous gulls.

## AND THEN THERE'S GLOOSCAP

As you stand on the cliff and fill your lungs with the sharp sea air, look to your right, across the brook where another cliff rises. There's another cave there. This one the Mi'kmaq's call *Kukmijnawe'nuk*, "place of my grandmother." They believe that the man-god Glooscap, having apparently had enough of the outside world, retired there with his grandmother. Another legend tells how Glooscap once tried to impress two maidens by leaping from his canoe to the shore, but the canoe broke in two on the rocks. The maidens laughed at his antics and he turned them both to stone—one on either side of the cave. If you look seaward you'll see what became of the broken canoe—we call them the Bird Islands.

Glooscap's cave, unfortunately, is not readily accessible to mere mortals, although some have managed to get to it by climbing down over the cliff. I don't recommend it. The cliffs are very unstable and dangerous.

The whole mountain, which rises behind you like a shield, is steeped in Indian legend. The ground itself is considered sacred and the fields and woods were once vital berry-hunting grounds. The trail is known as the Trail of the Little People and when the Mi'kmaq travelled through these woods they always walked single file out of respect for the "little people" and concern for the delicate balance of nature.

It's something to think about as you find a comfortable rock and unpack your well-deserved picnic lunch.

## Cape Dauphin

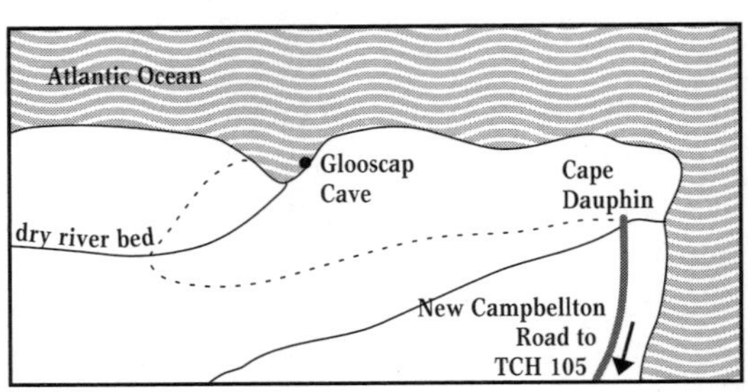


### DIRECTIONS

Just west of the Seal Island Bridge, on the Trans-Canada Highway, there's a hairpin turn at the base of Kelly's Mountain. About halfway around the turn is the road to New Campbellton. After about 18 km (11.1 mi) the road abruptly comes to an end. Park your car along the shoulder of the road.

**Activity**

Woodland hike to the ocean; exploring a cave.

**For Whom?**

Suitable for families with children over the age of five or six. Not suitable for the elderly or anyone with problems walking.

**Conditions and Terrain**

It can be damp underfoot. There are a few springs to cross. Trail is not groomed but defined enough to follow; occasional fallen tree to be walked around; a few uphill climbs; cave has a shallow opening but opens up inside.

**Distances**

Eighteen kilometres (11.1 mi) from Trans-Canada Highway to where you park your car. The trail is about 6 km (3.7 mi) return.

**Time Required**

The hike will take at least two hours, but you can plan to stay much longer, especially if you take along a picnic.

**Best Time of Year** Summer and fall.

**What to Wear/Bring**

Wear old sneakers or boots; take a jacket or sweater and insect repellent; bird/wildflower guide, flashlight optional.

**Special Features**

When you get to the coast you'll see the legendary Glooscap cave (or "fairy hole," as it's called). Birds, wildflowers, mushrooms, and other plants are abundant.

**Precautions**

Be careful on cliffs by the ocean. The rocks are very loose and dangerous. Watch children in cave.

**Facilities**

Gas station and restaurants on Sydney side of Seal Island Bridge.

## C2 THROUGH THE BROOK TO MACINTOSH FALLS

Most nature lovers would think nothing of tramping for hours through unknown woods, or picking their way down perilous cliffs, just to get close to a thundering waterfall. It seems that the more remote the location, the more intriguing the prospect.

Cape Breton has much to offer the waterfall fancier. Along the highways, or deep in

*Cape Breton has much to offer the waterfall fancier.*

the woods, waterfalls of all descriptions decorate the landscape like sequins, from Grand River to Cape North. And some, like the MacIntosh Brook Falls, offer to the adventurous traveller not only a magnificent waterfall, but an unforgettable walk along the way.

## GETTING THERE

Just before the village of Eskasoni, at a place called Island View, a brook runs down through a deep gorge, to Bras d'Or Lake. Because steep cliffs rise straight up from the brook like great stone walls, the trip to MacIntosh Falls—about 1 km (.62 mi) up the brook—must be made almost entirely by walking upstream, through the brook.

Now, walking a kilometre up a brook may not seem like a particularly pleasant way to spend an afternoon, but, oddly enough, it is. In fact, on a sunny warm day the journey up MacIntosh Brook is every bit as enchanting as the sight of the falls itself.

Once you come to the bridge, not far from the Island View sign, pull your car off the road and park there. Walk down over the bank to the brook. This is where the fun begins.

## UP THE BROOK

The best footgear for the walk is not boots, as you might imagine, but an old pair of sneakers with good traction. Boots will almost certainly get swamped before you reach the falls. I speak from experience when I say that wet sneakers can be quite tolerable and easy to walk in. Wet, sloshy boots are not!

So take off your socks, sling your knapsack over your back, and plunge your sneakers into the sparkling water of MacIntosh Brook.

You may want to break off some good sturdy alder branches for walking sticks. They help keep you upright.

As you pick your way upstream around a bend or two, you begin to feel the mountain closing around you like a hug. The cliffs hover overhead, letting nothing in from the outside world except the sunlight, and evergreens dangle from the cliffs filtering the rays into thin streaks, like stage lights. The depth of the water in the brook varies depending on the time of year and the amount of recent rainfall. Here and there you'll come upon pools that are deep enough to swim in, at least for children. On the way downstream they can drift along through the pools on the current. Although the pools aren't deep enough or large enough to pose a real danger, be sure not to leave children unattended. They'll thoroughly enjoy the "ride" downstream.

Further along you'll feel the brook beginning to slap against your legs with a little more gusto and notice that the ripple you've been hearing has escalated to more of a rumble. By the time you round the last bend and the soft mist starts to brush your face, you'll see and hear why you came. MacIntosh Brook Falls, even on a slow day, is a splendid sight.

As you approach you'll notice as well that the perpendicular cliffs have given way to a rocky, but much more negotiable, shoreline. Be careful as you ease your way up over the rocks to the falls. The pools at the foot of the falls are deep and can often form strong whirlpools from the force of the falling water. When the pools are calm, they are a delight to swim in.

So find a little cranny in the rocks, unpack your picnic, and enjoy the solitude only a spot like this—a short walk up a brook—can bring.

## MacIntosh Falls

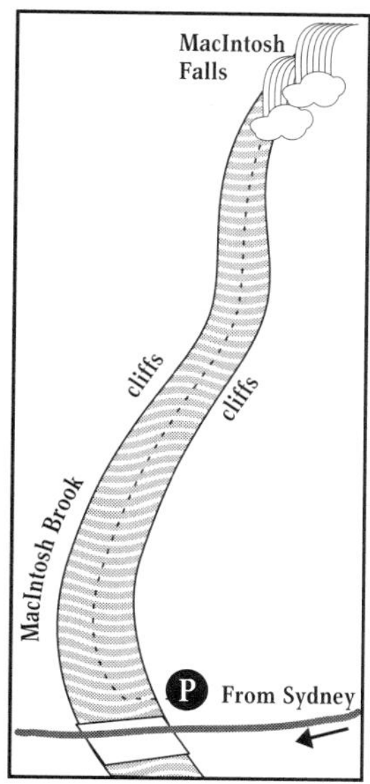


**DIRECTIONS**

Take Route 4 (from St. Peters or Sydney) to the turnoff to Eskasoni. Drive 14 km (8.7 mi) until you see the "Island View" sign on your right. Just past the sign (less than 1 km [.62 mi]) you'll come to a small white bridge over a brook. Pull your car off the road into the small clearing there, just before the bridge.

MACINTOSH FALLS • QUICK REFERENCE

**Activity**
A hike up a brook—through the brook!—to a magnificent waterfall; picnic and swim.

**For Whom?**
Not recommended for very small children, the elderly, or anyone with problems walking.

**Time Required**
Give yourself at least three hours for the hike, or plan to spend the day.

**Best Time of Year**
Late July, August, and September and even early October, if the weather stays warm. The fall colours are spectacular.

**Distances**
The drive from the Eskasoni turnoff to Island View is 14 km (8.7 mi); the walk up the brook is about 2 km (1.2 mi) return.

**What to Wear/Bring**
Shorts and/or bathing suit or long pants that you can roll up; towels, old sneakers (leave dry ones in the car), insect repellent; sunscreen; picnic, field guides optional.

**Special Features**
Brookside vegetation is abundant. There are birds and small animals all around. Swimming in the pools is fun, especially for children—the current will carry them along. Water is a very pleasant temperature despite it being a mountain brook.

**Precautions**
Walk cautiously, rocks in the brook can be slippery. Watch children carefully in the pools and if they climb on the rocks. Don't let them go too near the falls alone. Give yourself enough time to get back downstream before dark.

# HISTORY WALK THROUGH SYDNEY'S NORTH END

***The town is regularly planned, contains from sixty to seventy houses, rather handsomely built with gardens attached and a population of about 500.***

—John MacGregor, *British American,* 1832

Whether you're an architecture buff, a history nut, or a visitor just looking for a little local colour, you should treat yourself to a visit to Sydney's north end.

Within a few short blocks, you'll find enough history and intrigue to satisfy the most sophisticated sightseer. On Charlotte Street alone stand four houses and a church that were built in the 1700s. Two of the houses have been restored and are now public museums, and the church, once a garrison chapel, is open for visitors. Along the streets of Sydney's north end you'll discover wonderful samplings of architecture, from the simple Cape Cod style of early colonial days, to the classic revival and second empire styles of the mid and late 1800s.

So, if you'd like to get away from the traffic and hullabaloo for a few hours, park your car, put on your walking shoes, and come along on a stroll through history.

## ST. PATRICK'S MUSEUM

The best place to start is at St. Patrick's Church Museum (map #1), just north of York Street on the Esplanade. The original St. Pat's was built by a merchant named John Butler Wilson. His infant son, who died in 1798, still lies buried in the churchyard. The present church was built in 1828. It's a gothic-style gem, constructed from beautifully textured stone found on the island. The exhibits and artifacts there make it a perfect place to begin your tour and the guides will fill your head with images of the days when Sydney was known as *Cibou,* a Mi'kmaq word meaning "big river." They'll tell you about the loyalist settlers who built their simple homes from stone they scrounged from the abandoned ruins of the great fortress at Louisbourg.

Once you've soaked up some of the "colonial" atmosphere at St. Pat's, start walking north from the church along the Esplanade. Keep in mind that most of the houses on your walk have not been restored (yet!). But if you look closely, beyond the aluminum siding and picture windows, you may see the postmaster of 1870 handing out mail through his kitchen window at 37 Esplanade, or hear the bell on top of 54 Charlotte announce the dawn of another market day.

The house on the corner of Amelia, 53 Esplanade (map #2), was built in the 1850s. Its most remarkable feature is the five-sided "Scottish" dormers on the back—a very uncommon sight in this area. No one can explain this unusual feature.

Just north, number 43 (map #3), built in the early 1900s, was Sydney's first cement house; and number 37 (map #4), built in 1870, served as the colony's "kitchen-window" post office.

## VICTORIA PARK

Now walk just a bit further north, to DesBarres Street, and turn right. To your left is Victoria Park. When the Loyalist troops

# Sydney

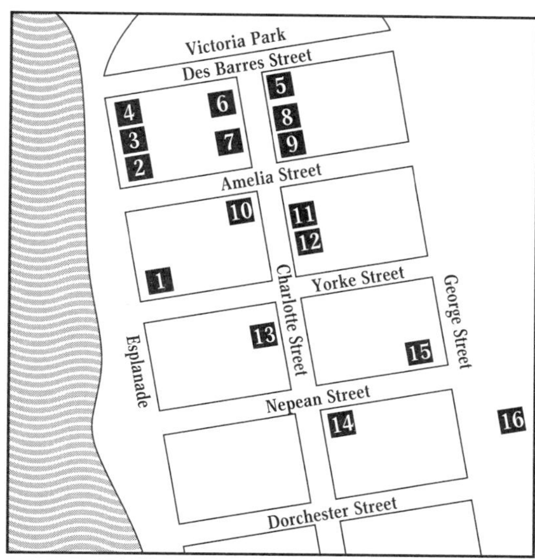


**1** St. Patrick's Church - originally built in 1798.

**2** 53 Esplanade - odd five-sided "Scottish" dormers.

**3** 43 Esplanade - Sydney's first cement house.

**4** 37 Esplanade - "kitchen window" post office.

**5** 3 Charlotte - built in 1897, recently owned by singer Rita MacNeil.

**6** 12 Charlotte - working man's house of coal and steel boom days, late 1800s.

**7** 24 Charlotte - built in 1860s, gables and widow's walk of sea captain's house.

**8** 25 Charlotte - Sydney's first courthouse and jail.

**9** 49 Charlotte - buit in 1902 as a "market house."

**10** 54 Charlotte - "Jost House," a museum.

**11** 75 Charlotte "Cossit House" - a museum, the oldest house in Sydney.

**12** 79 Charlotte - an old schoolhouse.

**13** 96-98 Charlotte - working class house of early 1800s.

**14** St George's Church - oldest Anglican Church in Sydney, built in 1785.

**15** Holy Angels Convent - girls school built in 1885.

**16** Lyceum - Centre for Heritage and Science.

landed here in 1785, their first concern was to defend their new home. Since this is the tip of the peninsula on which Sydney stands, it was the natural choice for a military installation—which, incidentally, was called Battery Park until Queen Victoria's diamond jubilee in 1897. After more than two hundred years, it is still used for military purposes.

### CHARLOTTE STREET

Walk up DesBarres Street to Charlotte and turn right. In 1795 this block, then a "suburb" of the main settlement, had to its credit only the customs house, the courthouse, and the gate to the governor's mansion. But by 1897, when 3 Charlotte (map #5) was built for a railway engineer, the block had become strictly residential. Except for the siding and a few small details, number 3 is very much as it was when it was built. Notice the odd mixture of bay windows on the front. (Perhaps that was what enticed singer Rita MacNeil to buy this house several years ago.)

The house at 12 Charlotte (map #6), just across the street, is a fine example of the very common "Greek revival" of the late 1800s and early 1900s, favoured by workers attracted to Cape Breton by the coal and steel boom. Simple, compact, and affordable, it was probably the "suburban bungalow" of the early 1900s.

Just up the street, number 24 (map #7) is a fascinating old house built in the 1860s. The peculiar roof line, with all the gables and what's left of a "widow's walk," conjure up images of the sea captain's wife, on a stormy fall afternoon, searching the sea for a sign of her husband's overdue ship. On happier occasions, the whole family might have watched as the arctic explorer Robert Peary tied up at the public wharf below to take on provisions for his latest expedition.

Cross the street again to number 25 (map #8), Sydney's first courthouse and jail, and imagine, if you can, the basement, dark and musty with tiny stone-walled cells and the dank smell of damp earth. This is where, in 1833, Charlotte Flahaven spent the last days of her life before she was led, proclaiming her innocence to the end, to Barracks Park, there to be hanged before a crowd of curious townsfolk, for the murder of her husband.

And when they weren't witnessing a hanging, the citizens of old Sydney might have been hustling toward 49 Charlotte (map #9), on the corner of Amelia, to haggle with a farmer over a sack of potatoes or a cut of beef. Number 49 was built in 1902 as a "market house"; later, after the market moved downtown, it became a fire station. The rooftop bell, which once summoned people to market, became a harbinger of disaster.

## JOST HOUSE

Cross over Charlotte again to the opposite corner. Number 54 (map #10) is known as Jost House and is one of the north end's treasures. It is a museum now and was restored to show its split personality. In some spots it's the Cape Cod "salt box" of the 1790s and in others it's the Newfoundland house of the early 1900s. The guides at Jost House will help you explore the house's colourful past; be sure to ask them about the basement.

## COSSIT HOUSE

The second of Sydney's historical jewels is 75 Charlotte (map #11). The Cossit House, across the street and a little south, was built in 1787 and is thought to be the oldest house in Sydney. Guides, dressed in the garb of the 1780s, will bring to life for you the days when Rev. Ranna Cossit, the first rector of St. George's Anglican Church, lived in this modest house with his large family.

*House on north Charlotte St., next to the Cossit House, c.1890.*

Next door, number 79 (map #12) was built a few years later in the same style as Cossit House and was probably used as a schoolhouse. The gabled second story was added later.

Less than ten years after the Reverend Cossit was sent to Sydney to attend to the spiritual needs of the king's subjects, the 33rd Regiment was shipped off to Halifax. For that and other reasons, the young colony all but became a ghost town until the turn of the century. Number 96–98 Charlotte (map #13)—

across the street and a little south—was then in its original form, typical of the working class housing built during Sydney's revival in the early 1800s. The low-pitched Newfoundland-style roof wasn't added until a century later.

**ST. GEORGE'S CHURCH**

Walk south just a little farther, to the corner of Charlotte and Nepean. On that corner stands St. George's Church (map #14), pretty much as it was when it was built over two hundred years ago. Once inside you'll have no trouble imagining a Sunday morning in 1787 and Reverend Cossit delivering a firey sermon on the evils of greed (possibly with political overtones) to a tightly-laced congregation that listens with all the sanctimony money can buy—the well-to-do in the front seats, the ordinary folk in the back. And today, some of those same citizens share the graveyard beyond the church walls.

Just across Nepean Street is Holy Angels Convent (map #15), a private girls school built by the Congregation of Notre Dame in 1885. It is to this day a girls school (public though, not private) and nuns still live in the convent part of the complex.

There's one final stop to make before you go back to the twentieth century. Walk up Nepean to George Street and turn right. Not far up George, on the opposite side, is the Lyceum (map #16), built in 1900 as Sydney's first cultural centre. On the bottom floor, the Centre for Heritage and Science will top off your tour. The exhibits there are always fascinating, and if any questions cropped up while you were walking, the guides will probably be able to answer them for you.

**DIRECTIONS**

Coming into Sydney from King's Road, keep left along the water (the Esplanade) and drive north until you come to the little stone church (St. Pat's) on your right.

Coming into Sydney from Louisbourg, stay on George Street (that's the Louisbourg Highway) until you come to Dorchester Street, in the far end of town. Turn left on Dorchester and drive down to the water and the Esplanade. Turn right on the Esplanade and drive north until you see the little stone church on your right.

SYDNEY • QUICK REFERENCE

**Activity**

Walking tour of the historic north end of Sydney, with visits to two restored houses and two museums.

**For Whom?**

Anyone interested in history and/or architecture.

**Time Required**

Allow at least two hours, but more time could be spent at the museums.

**Time of Year**

Summer and early fall.

**Special Features**

St. Patrick's Church Museum; Cossit House, Jost House, St. George's Church, the Centre for Heritage and Science, and the C.B. School of Crafts on the second floor of the Lyceum.

The central region of the island, as it is divided for the purposes of this book, encompasses almost all of Bras d'Or Lake. Here you will notice a significant personality change in the beaches. The shores of the Bras d'Or are not, of course, as wild and expansive as along the ocean, and you'll be more amidst grassy slopes and woods. The best part of Bras d'Or Lake's beaches is the water. Because it is lake water, it can be wonderfully warm in late July, August, and much of September. And for salt water lovers—no need to fret. The Bras d'Or is all salt water, although it's less salty than the ocean. Here are four highly recommended Bras d'Or beaches. Try them. You'll love them!

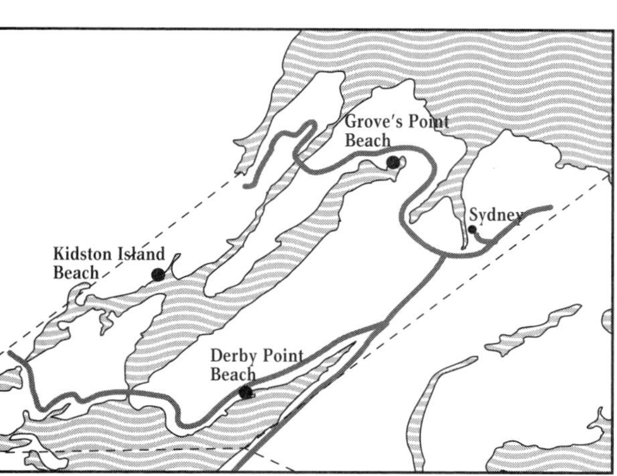


## GROVE'S POINT BEACH

This is really a park with lots of picnic tables on the hill and in among the evergreens. The beach itself is small, but it's sandy and shallow—great for children—and the water is warm.

### DIRECTIONS

Take the Trans-Canada Highway (Route 105) to Bras d'Or. Just west of the Bras d'Or Bridge, turn left at the FNS store to Grove's Point and South Side Boularderie. Drive down that road until you come to the park (about 5 km [3 mi]).

## DERBY POINT BEACH

(Near Grand Narrows)

This out-of-the-way spot is a glorious escape from reality. It's a wonderful sandy cove, surrounded by woods, beach grass, white cliffs, and, of course, the inviting, warm water of Bras d'Or Lake.

### DIRECTIONS

From Route 4 (St. Peter's or Sydney), take the turnoff to Eskasoni. Drive along that road, through Eskasoni, until you come to the sign to Derby Point (about 40 km [24.8 mi] from turnoff). Turn left onto Derby Road and drive about 3 km (1.9 mi) until you see the beach on your left. There's a road of sorts from the main road to the beach, but I suggest you walk. It looks a little unreliable for driving. From Iona, cross the new Barra Strait Bridge, then take the first right turnoff to Grand Narrows. Drive a short distance and turn right again. This takes you to the old ferry dock. Just before the dock is a gravel road—the Derby Road. Drive along until you see the beach, about 4 km (2.5 mi), just as you come over a steep hill.

## KIDSTON ISLAND BEACH

This island beach is just off the coast of Baddeck on Bras d'Or Lake. A boat service to the island runs all summer. The island is a lovely spot to spend a summer afternoon. You can swim or just stroll around the island. There is usually a canteen set up on the island.

**DIRECTIONS**

From the Trans-Canada Highway (Route 105), take one of the exits to Baddeck and drive into the centre of the village. Take the road that leads to the main wharf. The boat to the island leaves from the wharf.

Cape Breton Highlands National Park encompasses 950 square km (368.8 sq mi) of magnificent highlands and coastal wilderness stretching from Cheticamp on the Gulf of St. Lawrence to Ingonish on the Atlantic Ocean. It is a spectacular mixture of soaring mountains, plunging canyons, incredible beaches, and an intriguing highland plateau from which you can see gently rolling hills and broad valleys. Here the terrain is higher and more rugged than anywhere else in Nova Scotia.

Lucky for us the Cape Breton Highlands National Park is under the protection of Environment Canada's Parks Service. This means, we can hope, that it will be here to enjoy for many generations to come. It is one of the last remaining tracts of protected wilderness in Nova Scotia.

## THE TRAILS

One of the most exciting ways to experience the splendour of the Highlands Park is to feel it under your feet, above your head, and all around you. There are twenty-seven hiking trails in the park ranging from a twenty minute stroll along a rocky coast to a challenging mountain adventure. There are short flat trails, oceanside trails, mountain and plateau trails, woodland river valley trails, and wilderness camping trails. There's even a trail that is wheelchair accessible.

Here is a list of some of the twenty-seven hiking trails in the park. For a complete list and further information about the trails, ask for the booklet *Walking in the Highlands* at the Information Centres in Cheticamp and Ingonish.

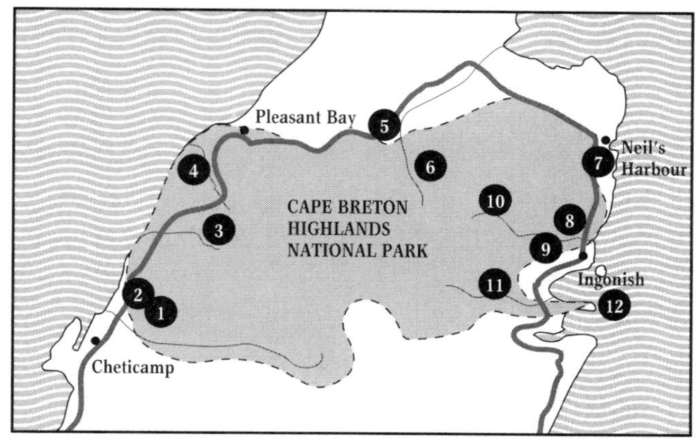


# Cape Breton Highlands National Park

| | | | |
|---|---|---|---|
| **1** | L'Acadien | **7** | Coastal |
| **2** | La Prairie | **8** | Broad Cove Mt. |
| **3** | Corney Brook | **9** | Warren Lake |
| **4** | Fishing Cove | **10** | Lake of Islands |
| **5** | Lone Shieling | **11** | Clyburn Valley |
| **6** | Aspy | **12** | Middle Head |

**L'Acadien** (begins at Cheticamp Information Centre): 9.6 km (6 mi) loop; 3–4 hours; Panoramic views of Cheticamp River Valley and coast; lookoffs and picnic spots.

**La Prairie** (just north of Information Centre in Cheticamp): 1.2 km (.75 mi) loop; 1/2 hour; name means "the meadow that borders the river as it reaches to the sea."

**Corney Brook** (9 km. north of Cheticamp): 8 km (5 mi) return; 2–3 hours; a dry level trail that explores mature hardwood forest of box canyon and ends at a small waterfall.

**Fishing Cove** (a few km south of Pleasant Bay): 16 km (10 mi) return; 4–5 hours; a steep trail down to a lovely cove and a wilderness camping site.

**Lone Shieling** (a few km east of Pleasant Bay): .8 km (.5 mi) loop; 20 min; you'll find a replica of a Scottish sheep crofter's hut surrounded by three-hundred-year-old sugar maples. Washrooms on trail.

**Aspy** (about midway between Pleasant Bay and Cape North): 9.6 km (6 mi) return; 3–4 hours; starts at Beulach Ban Falls and follows Aspy Valley then climbs to a lookoff.

*Offering spectacular scenery and a variety of trails, the Cape Breton Highlands Park is a must for outdoor enthusiasts.*

---

**Coastal** (just south of Neil's Harbour): 11 km (6.6 mi) return; 3–4 hours; a hike along cobble beaches; seabirds and whales are a likely sight.

**Broad Cove Mountain** (just north of Ingonish): 3.2 km (2 mi) return; 1 hour; a steep switchback trail to top of mountain with an eagle's view of Warren Lake and Atlantic Ocean. Bald eagles are frequently seen here.

**Warren Lake** (just north of Ingonish): 8.5 km (5.3 mi); 2–3 hours; a walk around Warren Lake with an abundance of interesting vegetation and wildlife.

**Lake of Islands** (accessible from Warren Lake Road, just north of Ingonish): 25.8 km (16 mi) return; 8–9 hours; threading around several bogs and across barrens, this old fire road ends at a primitive campsite; be prepared for muddy going and changeable weather.

**Clyburn Valley** (just north of Ingonish Beach): 9.2 km (5.7 mi) return; 2–3 hours; level and dry walking trail up Clyburn River to an abandoned gold mine.

**Middle Head** (just north of Ingonish Beach at Keltic Lodge): 4 km (2.5 mi) return; 1-1 ½ hours; walk around the peninsula with views of Cape Smokey and Tern Rock, nesting place for common and arctic tern. Tip of peninsula closed during nesting season.

If you've ever thought you'd like to delve into your family's genealogy but don't know where to begin—don't despair! Cape Breton historian and genealogist Jim St. Clair has compiled the following information to help you "dig up" your ancestors and get in touch with your Cape Breton roots.

Along with the scenery and recreational facilities, Cape Breton offers the visitor many opportunities for searching out ancestors. Thousands of people have left the Island of Cape Breton during the past two centuries. Their descendants are numbered in the hundreds of thousands and often come across the Canso Causeway with the expectation that they will find some trace of their great-grandparents.

It's useful to note that Cape Breton is a multi-ethnic place with immigrants coming from the United States, Quebec, Prince Edward Island, and many places in Europe and the Near East. In addition to the native Mi'kmaq inhabitants, the largest ethnic groups are the Irish, the Scots, the English who came as Loyalists, and the Channel Islanders. These groups often settled in identifiable communities amongst extended kinfolk.

## GATHER UP YOUR RECORDS

Before you begin your search, you should collect whatever records or information you may have about where your ancestors lived, and the dates of their birth, marriage, and death. Try to find family traditions such as occupations, nicknames, religious affiliation, or legends about mishaps or settlement pattern (lived next door to brothers or to people from Isle of Guernsey, for example). By searching in bureau drawers, old address books, photograph albums, or in the memories of older family members, you may find useful clues. Putting the known information on paper in some order is very helpful, both for the researcher and for local historians on Cape Breton.

## MAP AND PHONE BOOK

A good highway map with the names of communities and the four counties—Cape Breton, Inverness, Richmond, and Victoria—is a necessity. It is also helpful to consult a phone book (All the Cape Breton phone numbers are in one book and arranged by communities). If the name you are searching for is unusual, then the phone book may turn up relatives, but for many common names such as Smith, MacDonald, or Murphy, such a search is probably not useful.

## THE BEATON INSTITUTE AND OTHER ARCHIVES

The Beaton Institute at the University College of Cape Breton, located on the highway between Sydney and Glace Bay, is a good place to start your search. The archives are open during the day except on weekends. The staff will answer short questions on the phone but encourage people to come in and use the facilities. The 1871 Census is the most useful document for many people and may be consulted on microfilm at the Beaton. In addition, a large library of microfilm and print material is maintained at the Nova Scotia Highland Village at Iona, where the staff can give some help, particularly in the search for Scottish roots. The library and staff at Les

Trois Pignons in Cheticamp is particularly helpful if your family is of Acadian or French origin. Note that some names, such as Burke and Burns, seem to be Irish, but may in fact be French. A number of smaller archives like those at Cape North, Port Hood, Port Hastings, and Mabou have records that may be consulted.

The 1881, 1891, and 1900 Census records are now available for Cape Breton Island. These records can either be consulted here or through inter-library loan in many home locations. Birth and death records are provincial records only from 1864 to 1877. Churches kept records but they were sporadic. Marriage records were kept from 1864 to 1908 and may be seen on microfilm. Vital records after 1908 are found at the Deputy Registrar General's office, Box 157, Halifax, NS, B3M 2M9. Most school records are at the public archives in Halifax.

## CEMETERY AND COURTHOUSE RECORDS

Many of the cemetery records for the Island are also gathered at the Beaton Institute, along with the location of the graveyards. Other documents, such as petitions for land, deeds of land transfer, and wills—which county courthouses can provide—may also provide interesting information. The courthouse for Richmond County is in Arichat, for Cape Breton County in Sydney, for Inverness County in Port Hood, and for Victoria County in Baddeck. It is important to note that in Nova Scotia all "Mac" and "Mc" names are listed in such records as though the "Mc/Mac" did not exist. (For example, for MacNeil, look under Neil.)

## NETWORKING

Local historians can be found in almost all small communities and maintain an unofficial network. Ask the staff at the Beaton Institute or at any one of the other archives for the names and addresses of such people. Also, several researchers work for remuneration. You will find a listing for them at the Beaton Institute. Inverness County runs a query column in its monthly newspaper *The Participaper*. Address any queries you may have to The Editor, *Participaper*, Port Hood, Nova Scotia. The Nova Scotia Genealogical Society also publishes a journal, which may be seen at the Beaton, the Highland Village, and other archives. It too carries a number of queries. And, of course, don't forget just plain chit-chat. Many people in Cape Breton communities enjoy conversing with visitors, especially if those visitors have local roots, and much information can be obtained during a casual chat.

Genealogical searching on Cape Breton Island can often be frustrating, as the communities are widely separated and many records have been lost. But memories here are long, and the diligent researcher will often find good leads, which can be followed up through correspondence. At the worst, you'll meet some very friendly, helpful people who will try their best to assist you. Good digging!

## BY LOCATION

**BADDECK**
Uisge Ban Falls 49
Kidston Island Beach 154
**BRAS D'OR**
A Walk to the Caves at Cape Dauphin 136
Groves Point Beach 153
**CAPE NORTH**
A Walk Along Aspy Bay 37
Aspy Trail 158
**CHETICAMP**
L'Acadien Trail 157
La Prairie Trail 157
Corney Brook Trail 157
**DINGWALL**
Dingwall Beach 57
**DONKIN**
A Bird Walk Along Cape Perce 76
Fossil Hunting at Schooner Cove 66
**ESKASONI**
Through the Brook to MacIntosh Falls 140
**FOURCHU**
Morrison Beach 133
**FRAMBOISE**
Digging Clams at Fuller's Bridge 104
Overnight Camping at Framboise 109
Hike to Fox Cove 114
L'Archevesque Beach 131
**GABARUS**
Gabarus Beach 95
Belfry Beach 96
**INGONISH**
Broad Cove Mountain Trail 159
Warren Lake Trail 159
Warren Lake Beach 58
Lake of Islands Trail 159
**INGONISH BEACH**
Clyburn Valley Trail 159
Middle Head Trail 159

**INVERNESS**
Inverness Beach 22
**IONA**
Derby Point Beach 154
**ISLE MADAME**
A Walk Around Crichton Island 118
Road Tour of Isle Madame 123
Pondville Beach 130
**LAKE AINSLIE**
Egypt Falls 17
**LOUISBOURG**
Lighthouse Trail 70
Coastal Hike, Baleine 87
Coastal Hike, Gooseberry Cove 89
Kennington Cove Beach 93
**MABOU**
West Mabou Beach 22
**MAIN-A-DIEU**
Coastal Hike, Main-a-Dieu 85
**MARBLE MOUNTAIN**
A Day at Marble Mountain 98
**MARGAREE HARBOUR**
Margaree Harbour Beach 23
**MIRA**
Mira Gut Beach 94
**NEIL'S HARBOUR**
Coastal Trail 158
**NORTH RIVER**
North River Trail and Waterfall 32
**PLEASANT BAY**
Red River Trail 53
Fishing Cove Trail 157
Lone Shieling Trail 158
**PORT HOOD**
A Daytrip to Port Hood Island 12
Port Hood Beach 21
**PORT MORIEN**
Old French Mine 60
**ST. ANN'S**
A Craft Studio Tour 26

**ST. PETER'S**
Grand Greve Beach 131
Pt. Michaud Beach 133
**SYDNEY**
A Walk Through History 145
**TARBOTVALE**
Looking for Gold 41
A Visit to a Cold Spot 46

## TYPE OF ACTIVITY

**ADVENTURES**
Looking for Gold at Tarbotvale 41
A Visit to a Cold Spot 46
Fossil Hunting at Schooner Cove 66
A Bird Walk Along Cape Perce 76
Digging Clams at Fuller's Bridge 104
Overnight Camping at Framboise 109
A Walk to the Caves at Cape Dauphin 136
Digging Up Your Cape Breton Roots 160

**BEACHCOMBING/BEACH WALKS/ SWIMMING**
A Day Trip to Port Hood Island 12
A Walk Along Aspy Bay 37
Fossil Hunting at Schooner Cove 66
Lighthouse Trail 70
Main-a-Dieu 85
Baleine 87
Gooseberry Cove 89
A Day at Marble Mountain 98
Overnight Camping in Framboise 109
Hike to Fox Cove 114
A Walk Around Crichton Island 118
Beaches of the West 21
Beaches of the North 57
Beaches of the East 93

Beaches of the South 130
Beaches in the Central Part of the Island 153

## DISCOVERING NATURE

A Day Trip to Port Hood Island 12
Egypt Falls 17
North River Trail and Waterfall 32
Looking for Gold at Tarbotvale 41
Uisge Ban Falls 49
Red River Trail 53
Lighthouse Trail 70
Main-a-Dieu 85
Baleine 87
Gooseberry Cove 89
Digging Clams at Fuller's Bridge 104
Overnight Camping at Framboise 109
Hike to Fox Cove 114
A Walk Around Crichton Island 118
A Walk to the Caves at Cape Dauphin 136
Through the Brook to MacIntosh Falls 140

## HIKES - COASTAL AND LAKESIDE

Port Hood Island 12
Red River Trail 53
Lighthouse Trail 70
A Bird Walk Along Cape Perce 76
Main-a-Dieu 85
Baleine 87
Gooseberry Cove 89
A Day at Marble Mountain 98
Overnight Camping at Framboise 109
A Hike to Fox Cove 114
A Walk Around Crichton Island 118
Fishing Cove Trail 157
Coastal Trail 158
Warren Lake Trail 159
Middlehead Trail 159

**HIKES - WOODLAND**

A Day Trip to Port Hood Island 12
Egypt Falls 17
North River Trail 32
Looking for Gold at Tarbotvale 41
Uisge Ban Falls 49
Red River Trail 53
A Walk Around Crichton Island 118
A Walk to the Caves at Cape Dauphin 136
Through the Brook to MacIntosh Falls 140
L'Acadian Trail 157
La Prairie Trail 157
Corney Brook Trail 157
Fishing Cove Trail 157
Lone Shieling Trail 158
Aspy Trail 158
Broad Cove Mountain Trail 159
Lake of Islands Trail 159
Clyburn Valley Trail 159

**HISTORY EXCURSIONS**

A Day Trip to Port Hood Island 12
North River Trail 32
A Walk Along Aspy Bay 37
Old French Mine Site, Port Morien 60
Fossil Hunting at Schooner Cover 66
Lighthouse Trail 70
A Day at Marble Mountain 98
Road Tour of Isle Madame 123
History Walk Through Sydney's North End 145

**PICNIC PARKS**

North River Trail 32
A Walk Along Aspy Bay 37
Uisge Ban Falls 49
Main-a-Dieu 85
Road Tour of Isle Madame 123

**TOURS**

Craft Studio Tour, St. Ann's Bay 26
A Road Tour of Isle Madame 123

**WATERFALLS**

Egypt Falls 17
North River Trail and Waterfalls 32
Uisge Ban Falls 49
Through the Brook to MacIntosh Falls 140